Praying *the* Scriptures

A Field Guide for
Your Spiritual Journey

Evan B. Howard

InterVarsity Press
Downers Grove, Illinois

InterVarsity Press
P.O. Box 1400, Downers Grove, IL 60515
World Wide Web: www.ivpress.com
E-mail: mail@ivpress.com

InterVarsity Press® is the book-publishing division of InterVarsity Christian Fellowship/USA®, a student movement active on campus at hundreds of universities, colleges and schools of nursing in the United States of America, and a member movement of the International Fellowship of Evangelical Students. For information about local and regional activities, write Public Relations Dept., InterVarsity Christian Fellowship/USA, 6400 Schroeder Rd., P.O. Box 7895, Madison, WI 53707-7895.

Scripture quotations, unless otherwise noted, are from the New Revised Standard Version of the Bible, copyright 1989 by the Division of Christian Education of the National Council of the Churches of Christ in the U.S.A., and are used by permission.

ISBN 0-8308-2201-1

Cover photograph: Tony Stone Images

Printed in the United States of America ♾

Library of Congress Cataloging-in-Publication Data

Howard, Evan B., 1955-
   Praying the scriptures : a field guide for your spiritual journey
/ Evan B. Howard.
     p. cm.
   Includes bibliographical references.
   ISBN 0-8308-2201-1 (paper : alk. paper)
   1. Bible—Devotional use. 2. Prayer—Christianity. I. Title.
BS617.8.H68   1999
242'.5—dc21
                                          98-52769
                                            CIP

20	19	18	17	16	15	14	13	12	11	10	9	8	7	6	5	4	3	2	1
16	15	14	13	12	11	10	09	08	07	06	05	04	03	02	01	00	99		

Preface

I have drawn on the influence of many who have led me in the ways of praying the Scriptures, and to them this book owes a great debt. Bruce Gore first taught me how to pray the Lord's Prayer. The late pastor Keel Dresback inspired me to experiment with praying the Scriptures. The time my wife and I spent under the tutelage of Sr. Jean Rearden of the Fullerton Cenacle in Chicago has been of immense value in expanding our vocabulary of prayer. Chapters on the Psalms and on unanswered prayer were originally written as assignments for classes taught by Thomas McComiskey and Don Carson at Trinity Evangelical Divinity School. Their encouragement has been greatly appreciated. My exploration of Ignatian spirituality has been nurtured through the ministries of Fr. Bernard Tyrrell of Gonzaga University and Sr. Elizabeth Liebert of San Francisco Theological Seminary. My tenure at Vineyard Christian Fellowship of San Francisco has deeply enriched my sense of revival and deliverance prayer. Father Tom Belt from St. Paul's Episcopal Church in Montrose, Colorado, admirably modeled heartfelt and embodied worship. Many thanks to all!

The act of rewriting this book through its many drafts ultimately became a delightful community project. Jennifer Seidel took such care with an earlier draft that "doing a

Jennifer" has become our term for meticulous editing. The adult education class of St. Paul's Episcopal Church read one draft of the book, providing many helpful suggestions, as did Sandy Edwards of Hillcrest Congregational Church in Montrose. The editorial staff of InterVarsity Press has been very patient with this novice author. Much of the time spent in the editorial stage was financed through the generous supporters of Spirituality Shoppe. My two daughters, Claire and Terese, have provided formatting and artistic contributions at various stages. Finally, Cheri, my wife, has read the manuscript numerous times in various drafts. I am overjoyed and grateful to join with such a wonderful community of brothers and sisters.

Over the years our extended family has enjoyed making Christmas presents for each other. This book was developed first as a Christmas present especially for my father and my brother, in hopes that it might help support the prayers of the Howard homes. This book is therefore dedicated to Lawrence S. Howard and Keith S. Howard. May you have a merry Christmas and many wonderful hours of prayer thereafter.

Introduction
A Field Guide to Biblical Prayer

It all started when I was in seminary. I had prayed the Lord's Prayer and a few psalms before, but my habit of praying the Scriptures as a regular practice began while I was taking biblical Greek. Because the New Testament was written in Greek, my seminary required that students take this class to aid in interpreting the Scriptures. Our professor told the class that one way to absorb biblical Greek was to use the Greek text for our personal devotions.

I decided to try the idea. In fact, just for fun, I decided to locate, translate and meditate on all of Paul's prayers recorded in the New Testament. At first, all I could focus on were the strange words looking me square in the face. As I sat down for devotions, the odd verb tenses, long sentences and confusing vocabulary scattered across my page meant little to me. But as I made progress on my translations and began to move toward meditation, I began to explore something richer and deeper than just the Greek language.

I found myself entering the prayer life of the apostle Paul. I discovered the frequent thanksgivings that Paul lifted up to God as he dictated his letters to his secretary, words like "In our prayers for you we always thank God, the Father of our Lord Jesus Christ, for we have heard of your faith in Christ Jesus and of the love that you have for all the saints" (Colossians 1:3-4). I uncovered the requests that Paul lifted up before the Lord in his letters, requests like "And this is my prayer, that your love may overflow more and more with knowledge and full insight" (Philippians 1:9). I relished the spontaneous expressions of worship leaping at me out of Paul's most difficult theology, expressions like Romans 11:33, "O the depth of the riches and wisdom and knowledge of God! How unsearchable are his judgments and how inscrutable his ways!" In Paul's prayers I found better words than my own for my prayers of thanksgiving, requests and worship. I found myself repeatedly saying, "*That's* how I feel, God. He said it better than me."

Praying Paul's prayers hooked me. I wondered if other scriptural prayers would strike me in the same way, and I went on to Moses' prayers and David's. And so I began to make a practice of praying the Scriptures.

As I made praying the Scriptures a regular part of my devotions, I gained a great deal from this practice. Praying the Scriptures strengthened my confidence in prayer as I spoke to the Lord with words and attitudes reflected in his own Word. It brought power to my prayer as I identified with the intense emotions and the profound vision of God expressed by the writers of the Bible. It also stimulated personal change as my life and the texts of Scripture were brought into contact over and over again through prayer.

Through the years as I studied and experimented, I also collected. I collected different methods of praying the Scriptures, many of which turned out to be real winners. I also collected lists of Scriptures which were appropriate passages for use with the different methods of prayer. I have organized these methods and passages here in hope that others might be helped as I have been.

Let me begin by explaining just what I mean by *praying the Scriptures*. To pray the Scriptures is to order one's time of prayer around a particular text in the Bible. I might rewrite one of Paul's prayers of thanksgiving in my own words. I might meditate on a Gospel story. Or I might sing a psalm, or cry out in intercession for revival along with the prophets. In each of these examples a particular Scripture influences the words, mood and structure of my time with God.

I have found that one can use the Scriptures with every type of prayer; times of worship, confession, thanksgiving, intercession and meditation can all be structured around passages of Scripture. There are a number of reasons the Scriptures are so adaptable for use in prayer. First, the Bible itself is full of prayers. We find, for example, recorded prayers of Moses, Miriam, Isaiah, Elizabeth, Jesus and Paul, not to mention the wealth of prayers in the book of Psalms. If you are like me, sometimes you have trouble expressing yourself before God. You just can't seem to find the words to convey what is on your heart. Well, in the prayers of the Bible, you can find form for your prayers to God. And, by identifying with these *inspired* prayers, you acquaint yourself with prayer as God wants it prayed.

Second, quite often in some special way the Scriptures reveal to us the God to whom we come in prayer. To meditate on these passages is to conform our prayers to the character of God as God desires to be known. The stories of Jesus, for example, show us something of the character of the God we worship. I love the story of Jesus' meeting with Zacchaeus found in Luke 19. As I meditate on this passage, paying careful attention to the words, tone and actions of Jesus' encounter with Zacchaeus, I identify with Zacchaeus as he relates to Jesus. I am encouraged by Jesus' desire to befriend *me* and to receive *my* gifts to the poor. This type of meditation brings life to our prayer as Jesus engages us in fresh ways.

Third, some passages of Scripture reveal God's priorities to us, allowing our prayers to be conformed to God's concerns, and our lives to become conformed to our prayers. When I prayerfully read the apostle Paul's description of love in 1 Corinthians 13, I may be reminded of my own opportunity this day to avoid "being jealous or envious," and my prayers will reflect this concern. By regularly and prayerfully reflecting on these Scriptures, I may find the courage to practice the gospel of avoiding envy in the realities of my daily life.

I call this book a *field guide.* Our family loves the outdoors. While exploring the great outdoors we often find ourselves wanting to identify and to learn about the birds, trees and wildflowers in our area. So field guides have been our constant companions. A good field guide briefly helps the reader get acquainted with the subject, such as how-to's of bird identification. The field guide also gives lists, charts and pictures of a wide range of samples with more precise characteristics of identification (mallard, barn swallow, yellow-bellied sapsucker). These lists and pictures are often arranged by categories or families (ducks, swallows, woodpeckers).

This field guide for praying the Scriptures is arranged in a similar manner. The first part of the book, "A Guide to

Praying the Scriptures," is the how-to section. This part will help you get acquainted with the spirit and techniques of praying the Scriptures. It is divided into one chapter on the various prayer methods, eight chapters that roughly correspond to the primary categories of prayer and one last chapter on the question of unanswered prayer. These chapters are intended to be read in the beginning to gain an overview of ways to identify and use particular passages of Scripture in your times of prayer. They are not intended to give a comprehensive overview of all methods of praying the Scriptures; they are simply a collection of methods which have been helpful to me.

The second part of the book, "A Guide to Scriptures for Prayer," provides references to a wide range of specific biblical texts that can serve as material for your own biblical prayers. This part is divided into nine lists that roughly correspond to the main categories of prayer mentioned in the first part of the book. In the table of contents and at the beginning of each list I have identified which list belongs with which chapter. You may want to refer to these lists again and again to help you find passages to use in your times of praying the Scriptures.

My hope is that you will use this book to identify some of your own unspoken prayers. As I did, I hope that you too will explore the prayers of the Scriptures and find that they enrich your own thoughts, feelings and words as you pray.

PART 1

A GUIDE
TO PRAYING
THE SCRIPTURES

1

PRAYING THE SCRIPTURES

. . . .

One of the greatest attractions of praying the Scriptures is that *it is not boring*. The many different types of biblical passages lend their use to a variety of prayer methods. These methods engage heart, mind and body in our communication with God through the texts of the Bible. By becoming familiar with a few of these techniques, we can learn to match our own personality and mood to the passages of our Scripture prayers so that our devotional times become unique encounters with God. Here are a few of my favorite ways of praying the Scriptures.

Read Through the Passage Slowly
Slowly and quietly read through the passage. Think about every phrase, every word. When something strikes you, dwell on it for a while, then continue your reading. If something in the passage triggers communication to God, be attentive to what you want to express to him. Likewise be aware of what God may be saying to you through the pas-

sage. Try to get a feeling for the writer's meaning.

Sometimes you will find yourself identifying with the words of a passage in a new way. They cease simply to be passages from ancient texts and become your own words. You may discover that you pray the same words as the biblical writer, only now from the depths of your own being: "As a deer longs for flowing streams, so my soul longs for you, O God" (Psalm 42:1). The slow movement from text to prayer and back to text again forms a kind of rhythm that can hold your attention to God for some time and can stimulate special times of communication.

Some people have read through the entire Bible in this manner, listening for the voice of God in the text and voicing to him their prayers inspired by the text. At times God's voice pierces through a passage like a knife to their hearts. Others have been able to see the truths of their faith in new ways as they slowly read over old familiar passages. Still others have been inspired to new acts of love while slowly reading the stories of Scripture's heroes.

Read the Scripture Aloud

Sometimes it helps to read out loud. You may have a hard time focusing, or you may want to enter into the passage differently to catch something new. These are good times for reading aloud.

I like to try to read using the expression I think the author intended. By reading out loud in this way I retain more of the content and catch nuances I would not have otherwise noticed. I also allow my own identification with the passage to be expressed outwardly and concretely in my prayers.

Repeat a Phrase

At times the Holy Spirit will use a word or phrase to trigger your prayers. For example, you might read the phrase "for he has done marvelous things," and suddenly remember that you haven't thanked God for the way he's provided for your family lately. When a word or phrase strikes you like this, you may wish to repeat it again and again, either silently or aloud. You repeat, "He has done marvelous things; you have done marvelous things," perhaps spending the rest of your prayer time thanking God for his provision. This is not an unusual practice in Christian prayer. The Hebrew words for *meditate* suggest a background of "muttering," perhaps taken from the practice of reading aloud one's Scripture lessons over and over. Through this muttering you can reflect simultaneously on the words, the meaning and the application of a small bite-sized piece of Scripture.

Identify with the Emotions

When no specific word or phrase gets your attention, sometimes a feeling will. As you read and pray over a passage of Scripture, you may experience joy, repentance, grief, love or some other emotion. This feeling may be a communication to you *from* God, perceived *through* your own feelings. Likewise feelings *toward* God can be triggered by the emotive tone of the passage you are praying.

In a church prayer meeting a friend of mine was reading and praying through the book of Isaiah. Gradually, a deep sense of compassion for the church overwhelmed him. Tears ran down his cheeks as he prayed for the body of Christ. He found himself sharing the heart of the God who says, "Can a woman forget her nursing child, or show no compassion for the child of her womb? Even these may forget, yet I will not forget you" (Isaiah 49:15). The emotions of the passage merged with his own in prayer as he identified with the heart of the text.

The best way to cultivate this identification is to talk honestly to God using the words of the Scripture. Listen to God through the passage; be present with God through the passage. Do not let yourself get bogged down with method; rather be free to be with God. Try not to force or to suppress your emotions as you read and pray. Just give yourself over to the full understanding of the text and the full expression of yourself before God, and let the rest simply come. Identify with the passage: get into its emotional tone and become conscious of its perspective of God. Ask yourself, "What may the writer have been feeling while penning these words?" Allow yourself to be drawn into fervent prayer or deep meditation. As you begin to share the feelings of the Scriptures, your prayers will begin to express the heart of the God who inspired them.

Use a Commentary
Sometimes when I am reading through a passage or pondering a phrase I get stuck. I just don't understand what it could mean. Such was the case with Psalm 133, which reads,

How very good and pleasant it is
    when kindred live together in unity!
It is like the precious oil on the head,

running down upon the beard,
on the beard of Aaron,
  running down over the collar of his robes.
It is like the dew of Hermon,
  which falls on the mountains of Zion.
For there the LORD ordained his blessing,
  life forevermore.

I just could not see what oil running down some guy's beard had to do with kindred dwelling in unity. Not wanting to interrupt my quiet time by spending an hour studying the passage in detail, I simply took a few minutes to look up it in a brief commentary. The explanation said that Aaron's oil was the oil of anointing, a symbol of God's blessing. This blessing is not limited to the top of the head, but reaches from the top of the head even to the robes. This blessing is also like the dew which comes from Hermon (at the northernmost border of Israel) and falls on Zion (in the south). The experience of unity is likewise unlimited. It reaches a great distance encompassing a wide variety of people. God's blessing of life is richly experienced when people of wide differences share the same grace of God. Having thus briefly glanced at a commentary, I was able to return to my prayers for the unity of God's people with better understanding and more vigor.

Sing It

In the past few decades there has been something of a resurgence of Scripture singing in the church. Praise songs and Scripture choruses set to Bible verses abound. It's often refreshing to listen to recordings of these during devotional times. Why not try to sing a few along with the recording or even without accompaniment? Find a place and a time where you can sing as loud as you want and go for it! Many people use the privacy of their automobile for this purpose.

Rewrite It
What? Rewrite Scripture? No, just put it in your own words. This could take the form of a loose paraphrase or of an actual prayer that expresses the sentiment of the passage. Here is Psalm 137:1-6 as written:

> By the rivers of Babylon—
>   there we sat down and there we wept
>   when we remembered Zion.
> On the willows there
>   we hung up our harps.
> For there our captors
>   asked us for songs,
> and our tormentors asked for mirth, saying,
>   "Sing us one of the songs of Zion!"
>
> How could we sing the LORD's song
>   in a foreign land?
> If I forget you, O Jerusalem,
>   let my right hand wither!
> Let my tongue cling to the roof of my mouth,
>   if I do not remember you,
> if I do not set Jerusalem
>   above my highest joy.

This prayer captures the same sentiment of the psalm:

Lord, when I remember all you wanted to give your
people,
  and how they disobeyed,
  and how you brought them far from their home,
And when I think of all you want for me
  and how far from that I feel now, I want to cry.
I know we are to be joyful and full of song,
  but I just don't feel like singing.
How can I sing your songs, Lord, in this urban place
  that seems so far from you?
Help me, O Lord, as I live in this environment so hostile to
  you,
  to never forget you and to keep you as my highest joy.

In addition to writing out prayers to God in your own words, you may wish to write out the words that you hear God speaking as you read or write your prayer.

Add a Name

A simple method of rewriting is to add a name to the passage. Simply replace the passage's more general reference for a specific name or names that may be significant for you at the moment.

Ephesians 3:16-19 reads:

I pray that, according to the riches of his glory, he may grant that you may be strengthened in your inner being with power through his Spirit, and that Christ may dwell in your hearts through faith, as you are being rooted and grounded in love. I pray that you may have the power to comprehend, with all the saints, what is the breadth and length and height and depth, and to know the love of Christ that surpasses knowledge, so that you may be filled with all the fullness of God.

In response we might write:

I pray that, according to the riches of your glory, Lord, you may grant that Joe be strengthened in his inner being with power through your Spirit. Lord, you know how he needs this strength right now. I pray that Christ might dwell in his heart through faith, as he is rooted and grounded in love. I pray that Joe has the power to grasp with other Christians what is the breadth and length and height and depth, and that he really knows the love of Christ that surpasses knowledge, so that Joe will be filled with all the fullness of God.

Simply adding a name can transform a passage into a personalized prayer.

Do It

As your voice begins to express its deepest longings through Scripture, the Spirit will also communicate to you, through the very passages of your prayer times, Christ's deepest longings. Your concerns and God's concerns will merge as you spend time with the inspired words of Scripture in prayer. As this happens, there will come times when the natural extension of your prayer is action.

Indeed, often part of the prayer time itself is the reflection of your life in light of the Scriptures. As you slowly read the story of Jesus washing the disciples' feet, you may be moved to humility in your own life. You identify with Paul's prayer of thanksgiving for the generosity of the Philippian saints and are inspired to explore specific acts of thanksgiving and generosity yourself. Some of this exploration will occur during the prayer time itself, as you envision your life in conformity with the passages you pray.

Sometimes the movement toward action from Scripture praying will be easy and natural, as if you are being invited into something you always have sought. At other times God's invitation will not be so easy to accept. You will be called out of your comfort zone and asked to confront matters you would rather avoid. In such times of invitation, whether easy or difficult, praying the Scriptures must find expression in embodying the Scriptures.

While I would like to promise that praying the Scriptures will always make prayer times happy and enriching, I can't. Many times they are—the Scriptures you pray may bring you into joys never experienced and even usher you into the very glory of God. But sometimes encounters with God through the Scriptures can bring great pain and sorrow. You may cry with God through the prophets for the complacency of God's people. You may discover your own rebellious heart through praying an enemy psalm or experience an awkward tension in your relationship with God because you are afraid or unwilling to face the pain of transformation. You may cry out in a time of need, calling on God according to the promises of Scripture, only to feel the apparent rejection of unanswered prayer. You will feel keenly both God's pleasure and God's pain through praying the Scriptures.

My aim in introducing you to praying the Scriptures is not that all your prayer times become fulfilling. I hope and expect that many will be. But more important, I hope that I can help your prayer times to become more real. I hope that through the good times, the bad times and the so-so times, the practice of praying the Scriptures may provide the means by which you can more clearly speak to God, hear God and simply be present with God.

Remember, just as good communication with a friend or spouse requires time and experimentation, so also your prayer life needs time and practice. Feel free to give your prayers with Scripture some time for development. Try out a few favorite Scriptures, or, better yet, practice them with the various types of Scripture prayers as presented in the following chapters.

2

THE MODEL PRAYER OF OUR LORD

"PRAY THEN LIKE THIS."

I remember the month I spent living in a tent in rural Minnesota, waiting for the union job that would pay my way through the next year of college. The job never came, but I had a wonderful month playing pioneer, reading books and visiting with friends.

One special part of that month was my leisurely devotional time with God in the mornings. Since I didn't have to go anywhere early in the day, I lay in my sleeping bag, avoiding the mosquitoes that were waiting to have me for breakfast if I ventured out. And because there wasn't any room to read or write, I didn't try any fancy methods of prayer.

Every morning I simply prayed through the Lord's Prayer phrase by phrase. I found that going through just that one prayer allowed me intervals for worship, surrender, request and confession. Sometimes it took quite awhile to work my way through the whole prayer. By the time I finished, though,

I was ready to brave the mosquitoes and whatever else my day would bring. Those were precious times with God. Through them the practice of praying the Lord's Prayer became an established part of my walk with God.

The Lord's Prayer, sometimes referred to as the "Our Father," has long been recognized as the most important prayer in the Scriptures and is the most frequently spoken prayer in the Christian faith. When the disciples asked, "Lord, teach us to pray," Jesus taught them this prayer (Luke 11:2-4). We know it best as it is worded in the Revised Standard Version of Matthew 6:9-13.

Pray then like this:

Our Father who art in heaven,
Hallowed be thy name.
Thy kingdom come,
Thy will be done,
  On earth as it is in heaven.
Give us this day our daily bread;
And forgive us our debts,
  As we also have forgiven our debtors;
And lead us not into temptation,
  But deliver us from evil.

The Lord's Prayer was meant to be a simple model for ordinary prayers. Look at the beginning of the prayer again. Did Jesus tell his disciples, "You should pray four times a day," "You should pray a lot" or "You should pray like St. Francis"? No, he simply says, "Pray then like this." By proposing the wording of the Lord's Prayer in this manner, Jesus presents his followers, both past and present, with a wonderful pattern for prayer. While we need not always repeat the exact words of the Lord's Prayer, its themes give us the basic structure of our own prayers, suggesting the types of things we might pray for. And because the Lord's Prayer is presented in the first person plural (*our* Father), it is meant to be used both in our prayer for ourselves and for others.

Following Jesus' Model

A simple way to pray the Lord's Prayer is to follow the structure of the prayer in a devotional time just as I did. It is especially good as a prayer to begin the day.

To use it in personal devotions, first repeat a phrase of the prayer and then generalize the theme of that phrase for yourself or others.

Worshiping God. "Our Father who art in heaven, hallowed be thy name." Urging that the Lord's name be "hallowed" (or honored), proclaiming the specialness of God, is worship. So after repeating this phrase you should spend time worshiping him. You might thank God for what he has done, praise God for who he is or honor God for his character. It is helpful here to be specific. You might tell Jesus just how wonderful it is to know you are accepted by him even when it seems others don't accept you. You might let the Lord know you are glad his plan for the world is bigger than the world's plans, especially when the plans of government or society seem faulty. After spending a few moments honoring God you may go on to the next phrase.

Surrendering to God's will. "Thy kingdom come, thy will be done." This passage reflects a desire for God's rule to be present on the earth and in our lives. It is a longing for and a submitting to that rule. So after praying this phrase you would ask God to reign over those areas of your life or others' lives that come to mind. You know those areas that are in special need of the Lord's rule on a given day. "Lord, I pray that you would become the ruler of our family," you might pray. "I want our quarreling and cruel behavior to stop so that we will show that you are the King of our house." You might pray also for the church or for your neighborhood. Or you could pray for the secret places in our hearts that are hard to surrender to the King: "Lord, let your kingdom come into my jealous heart today." Having looked at your life from God's perspective, you are ready to move on to the next phrase.

Making necessary petitions. "Give us this day our daily bread." At the recitation of this phrase you call to mind the needs of the day. Are you in good health? God cares about your health and wants to hear about it. Are you in need of comfort, friendship or meaning? Ask the Lord. Now is the time to be honest with God. And as you need, so you ask. What is your "daily bread" today?

I love this time in my prayers. "Lord," I pray, "now here we are in a new town, after all this planning. I've been dreaming about living here for some time. But I'm scared I can't do it. I need confidence, Lord. It feels like I'm no good at anything. Help me. Remind me of who I am and why I came here." I tell God my needs, both real and imagined. Then I sit awhile, and God talks to me about my needs.

In a similar manner I tell God about the needs of others. I like this too, for in prayer I can tell God exactly what I think of someone, and the Comforter will listen. I tell God what I think someone's needs are. Then I listen as God tells me a few of the things about that person that he feels.

Confessing sins. "Forgive us our debts, as we also have forgiven our debtors." With this phrase think back over the past day and examine yourself. Did you do battle with those sins against which you so sincerely wanted to fight? On which battlefields did you slip and fall? Confess those sins right away, and receive God's forgiveness. Perhaps God will offer helpful hints for the next time you face a similar situation.

Is there someone who offended or injured you recently, whom you have not forgiven? Again, now is the time to forgive this person and receive the cleansing of the Lord. "O Lord," you might say, "my boss is a total jerk. All she thinks about is those performance charts. When she spoke about my lack of productivity in the meeting yesterday in front of everybody, that hurt, and I'm angry. But you ask me to forgive her, Lord. So I do. I'll just forget about this and try to do the best that I can, even if she doesn't notice the real work I do for the company."

Seeking deliverance from evil. "And lead us not into temptation, but deliver us from evil." You know the temptations you will be facing on a given day. You know where the flesh, the world or the devil may try to grab you and pull you down. So you might pray, "Today, Lord, I am going to walk right by the bakery on the way to school. And you know, Lord, how much I like chocolate cream-filled doughnuts. And Lord, when I go past the bakery it will be 8:00 a.m., and those chocolate cream-filled doughnuts will be sitting freshly made on the counters. And as usual, Lord, the doors of the bakery will be opened, and I don't think I can resist the smell. Help me, Lord! Give me the strength to just walk on by." Whatever the temptation, we pray a similar prayer so God will strengthen us.

You also can offer a deliverance prayer for family, friends or neighbors. "God, I pray for the kids of the Prodigal Project ministry who are going through withdrawal. These kids going off drugs certainly need your delivering power. Remove the influence of the enemy from their lives and establish your kingdom in these kids." Offering deliverance prayer on behalf of others can strengthen them against their weaknesses.

Coming full circle. Some believers commonly end the Lord's Prayer with the declaration "For thine is the kingdom and the power and the glory forever. Amen." If you add this phrase, you return to worship once again—a perfect way to close the prayer.

And so in this manner you move through the prayer, phrase by phrase, hallowing the name of the Lord (worship), giving your life over to God's rule (surrender), asking for the needs of the day (petition), admitting what you have done wrong (confession) and asking for help in troubled areas (deliverance).

"Pray like this," Jesus says. In this suggestion are the foundation stones for a prayer life worth living. By including in our times of prayer the elements suggested by the Lord's Prayer, we can find a simple, yet solid, model for our practice of prayer. In LIST A I have given a chart (from the Revised Standard Version) that presents this use of the Lord's Prayer.

3

PRAYING
THE PSALMS

....

"I WILL LIFT MY EYES TO THE LORD."

The Psalms have been at the heart of Christian prayer throughout the church's history. The epistle to the Ephesians encourages believers to "be filled with the Spirit, as you sing psalms and hymns and spiritual songs among yourselves, singing and making melody to the Lord in your hearts" (Ephesians 5:18-19). The earliest leaders of the church quote from the Psalms more frequently than from any other Old Testament book. For over one thousand years men and women in monasteries throughout the Christian world placed such importance on the Psalms that they systematically chanted them such that the entire book would be sung weekly. When the American Pilgrims ventured into publishing, the first volume they printed was the *Bay Psalm Book*, a metrical translation of the Psalms. Virtually all denominational books of prayer and worship have had selections of psalms for use in prayer. In recent decades we have seen a renewal of interest in the psalms; numerous praise songs have been based on them. Quoted, chanted, published, prayed and sung, psalms are favorites valued by every generation of Christian believers.

The Value of the Psalms

The Psalms have this enduring value for a few key reasons. First, most of the psalms in the Bible are uniquely inspired prayers and therefore are models of prayer for believers. By acquainting ourselves with them we come to know the structure and content of prayer as God wants it prayed. For example, many of us encounter times when we feel forgotten by God and perhaps do not know how to pray. It is good in times like these to be led through the phrases of Psalm 13. How wonderful to be able to cry out to God ("How long, O LORD? Will you forget me forever?"), to pursue the Lord in prayer ("Consider and answer me, O LORD my God!") and finally to regain our trust in him ("But I trusted in your unfailing love; my heart shall rejoice in your salvation"). God has provided these psalms as models so that we will know how to approach him in prayer.

Second, psalms are valuable because they express the full range of human emotion (as LIST B shows). Psalms range from quiet worship, "I have calmed and quieted my soul, like a weaned child with its mother" (131:2), to loud praise, "God has gone up with a shout, the LORD with the sound of a trumpet. Sing praises to God" (47:5-6). They express deep sorrow, "I am weary with my moaning; every night I flood my bed with tears; I drench my couch with my weeping" (6:6), and even fierce anger, "Happy shall they be who pay you back what you have done to us! Happy shall they be who take your little ones and dash them against the rock!" (137:8-9). We can identify with psalms in all of our various moods and situations. In them we see that no emotional expression is forbidden before God.

Third, the book of Psalms provides us with some of the clearest pictures of who God is and how he relates to his people. By looking at the various ways the psalmist pictures God, we can begin to find our own image of God enlarged. For example, reflecting on Psalm 93 ("The LORD is king, he is robed in majesty; the LORD is robed, he is girded with strength.... More majestic than the waves of the sea, majestic on high is the LORD!"), we are confronted with a picture of the powerful Lord God. If we cultivate this picture of the Lord with us in a morning meditation and carry it with us throughout the day, we are certain to approach our day from a position of strength. We know we have a mighty God with us!

How to Pray the Psalms

Many of the methods outlined in chapter one are ideal for use with the Psalms. Here are a few of my favorites, along with a couple of methods especially suited to the Psalms.

Rewrite them. Psalms are perfect for rewriting in your own words. You can find encouragement from a practice of taking psalms and rewriting them in light of a given situation. You might wish to turn a psalm into a letter to God, communicating exactly how you feel about things.

Sing them. Since many of the psalms are *songs*, singing is a wonderful method of praying the psalms. During my first year as a Christian, I was in my school's ninth-grade choir.

The teacher taught us "The New Twenty-third," a musical arrangement of Psalm 23. I thought it was fabulous to sing this psalm to God in school. I was thrilled each time the teacher pulled out the music for us to practice. It would be running through my mind for the rest of the day. Having this song, this psalm, on my mind was an act of prayer in itself. As I have mentioned, praise songs and Scripture choruses, many of them based on the Psalms, are readily available for your enjoyment and use in your devotional life.

Use their poetic structure as a model. What is most distinctive about the book of Psalms in Scripture is that it is a book of *poems.* As poetry, psalms are written with a particular structure, a structure that can direct the progress of your approach to God.

Some, like Psalm 22, begin with an angry *complaint* to God: "My God, my God, why have you forsaken me?" (v. 1). Then comes a *description* of the situation that grieves the writer: "All who see me mock at me . . . My hands and feet have shriveled" (vv. 7, 16). This description of the situation is presented alongside verses that *remind* the writer (and God) of God's own character: "Yet you are holy, enthroned on the praises of Israel. . . . It was you who took me from the womb" (vv. 3, 9). The writer then makes a request or *plea* to God: "O my help, come quickly to my aid! Deliver my soul from the sword" (vv. 19-20). Finally, in the heart of the writer there comes a *resolution,* and the psalmist ends with praise: "You who fear the LORD, praise him! All you offspring of Jacob, glorify him" (v. 23).

It is easy to find in this basic pattern—complaint, description, reminder, plea, resolution—a model for our own prayers. While this particular pattern is not the only one in the Psalms, it illustrates the way they are structured poetically according to natural progressions of human expression. By looking for the poetic structuring of the psalms you pray, you will find helpful frameworks for the expression of your own prayers to God.

Reflect on their images. As poetry, the Psalms are especially rich in imagery. "Blessed be the LORD, my rock," declares Psalm 144, "my rock and my fortress, my stronghold and my deliverer, my shield, in whom I take refuge." This poem piles up powerful metaphors to give the reader a feel for the character of God: rock, fortress, stronghold, deliverer, shield. Rich poetic images like these were not written simply to teach facts about God. Rather, like all good poetry, they are meant to guide the mind to see something in a new way. Let your mind wander as you reflect on these images. Have you ever seen a fortress? What comes to your mind when you think of fortresses? How is God like a fortress? How is he different? Let your mind play with images as they are given in Scripture. This is what poetry is all about. You may well find that by your enjoying the richness of the poetic expression in the Psalms your own prayers are enriched.

Let them touch heart as well as mind. As both poetry and song, the Psalms were intended not simply to inform the mind, but to inspire the heart in approach to God. As I mentioned in the beginning of this chapter, one of the values of psalms is that they express the full range of human emotion. Developing the skill of identifying with the emotional content of a passage might be a new exercise for many of us. We may have read our Bibles only as a book providing information or direction for life. I know this tendency well. I have become convinced, however, that God intended Scripture, and especially the Psalms, to be grasped not only by understanding the concepts of the text but also by a heartfelt identification with the feelings of the text. It is well worth the effort simply to sit with a text for a while, allowing the feelings conveyed in the passage to kindle or express your own feelings.

As we begin to sincerely pray the Psalms in our times of devotion, we will begin to take on the faith and perspective of the psalmists that have made this book so central in Christian life and history, and in so doing, our own lives will be enriched.

One type of psalm you will discover as you begin to explore praying the Psalms is the "enemy psalm." Because enemy psalms are so common, because they are so difficult for us to identify with in prayer and because they directly address the topic of deliverance prayer, I have covered them separately in chapter nine.

LIST B presents a guide to the various psalms that can be prayed in different seasons of life. "Psalms Listed by Mood" lists categories that reflect the variety of emotions and circumstances both of the Psalms and our own lives. As you begin your time of prayer, just choose the category that best suits your mood. To the right of the category is a list of psalms that serve to express that sentiment.

4

WORSHIP, PRAISE
& THANKSGIVING
WITH THE
SCRIPTURE

....

*"OUR FATHER WHO ART IN HEAVEN,
HALLOWED BE THY NAME."*

When I was a child, I worshiped my parents and Santa Claus. I didn't bow before them and offer sacrifices (apart from the cookies we put on the hearth for Santa on Christmas Eve), but deep inside I was aware that my parents held total authority over my life and that Santa, who knew whether I had been bad or good, gave me great gifts if I was good. I respected them, I admired them, and I was dependent on them. When they rescued me from a scrape, gave me good things and took me where I wanted to go, I was thankful.

I remember one occasion in particular. My father and I were camping, and I had just lost his favorite fishing pole by "casting" it into the lake. Instead of harshly reprimanding me, he tied fishing line to a stick and promptly caught a fish. At the time I would not have called my appreciation *worship*, but the combination of dependence, admiration and sense of my dad's greatness truly was expressive of what we call *worship*.

Everybody worships. Indeed, the acts of worship and thanksgiving are basic to the human person. Although we are seldom conscious of it, our sense of smallness before something greater, and our gratitude to that something for life, shape the very form of our existence. The way we worship our parents when we're young is merely a hint of a much greater and deeper sense of admiration and dependency in relationship with that *Someone* who is the almighty God. Yet because this sense of worship and admiration is so basic and deep, our sense of worship for God is not always conscious or expressed. It is easy, however, to learn to express worship and praise to God, especially when we receive such good gifts from him.

We have already seen in chapter two how important worship is to Christian prayer. The recognition of the Lord's character and the desire for the Lord's name to be hallowed, to be recognized as supremely special, form the first sentence of Jesus' model prayer. Likewise, we have found that the book of Psalms is full of songs of worship, praise and thanksgiving. Worship and praise for who God is and for what our Maker has done in creation or in history, thanksgiving for God's care and provision, gratefulness for answered prayer—all are richly represented in the book of Psalms. Praying the Lord's Prayer and the Psalms can cultivate our sense of worship and thanksgiving to God.

In addition, we can pray many different parts of Scripture to give voice to our own times of worship and thanksgiving. These prayers can be divided into two primary types: passages that are prayers of worship or praise in themselves and passages that provide a picture of worship that can enrich our own prayer.

Scriptural Expressions of Worship
Many books of the Bible record prayers of worship or praise. Moses sings of God's victory in Exodus 15. David praises the Lord when he is rescued from the hand of Saul in 2 Samuel 22. The apostle Paul includes a number of worship songs and thanksgivings to God in his letters. Even the book of Revelation contains worship and praise prayers.

Biblical prayers of worship and thanksgiving provide words for your own worship and thanksgiving. All you need to do is personalize the prayers. The methods (discussed in chapter one) of reading, repeating, rewriting, adding names and identifying with the text's emotion all work very well. You might choose, for example, to pray Paul's benediction found in (1 Timothy 1:17):

To the King of ages, immortal, invisible, the only God, be honor and glory for ever and ever. Amen.

It is simple to transfer the sense and emotion of the passage into your own words, declaring them to God as did Paul:

O Lord, you are the ruler over everything.
You always have been. We die, but you don't.
You have always lived, and you will always live.
You are awesome.
No one has seen you, for you are invisible.
Even though others live their lives for many things,

> *you are the only real God.*
> *I am so impressed with you. Amen.*

It's easy to let the tone and words of biblical passages shape your prayers as you meditate.

I loved the way Mark worked and worshiped. Mark was a friend with whom I painted on a few construction jobs in San Francisco. He always brought his prayer time into his work. Whenever possible he would carry a tape recorder to the job site and play worship music. The words of the songs, frequently directly from the Scriptures, created a holy atmosphere in our workplace. Often he would sing with the music; on one occasion all of us who were on the job sang at the top of our lungs. Even if the music was turned off, a phrase or two from the songs would still wind its way in and out of our minds and mouths, keeping the atmosphere of worship present.

Listening to worship music is simple and enjoyable, and a song is a kind of prayer that you can keep with you for the rest of the day. At times you may even like to listen to a song over and over again so that you can soak in the message and then take it with you throughout the day.

Scriptural Windows on Worship

Other passages of Scripture are not prayers of worship, but they give us a picture of worship that can inform our own worship.

Isaiah writes, "I saw the Lord, sitting on a throne, high and lofty; . . . The pivots on the thresholds shook. . . . And I said, 'Woe is me! For I am lost; for I am a man of unclean lips, and I live among a people of unclean lips; yet my eyes have seen the King, the LORD of hosts!' " (Isaiah 6:1, 4-5). One cannot read this passage without being transported into Isaiah's experience. In reading the passage you see the majestic throne on high. Can't you feel the building shake? Can't you sense the brokenness of Isaiah before the almighty God?

In a similar manner, by reading the New Testament story of the ten lepers you may be drawn to return to Jesus and give him thanks for his kindness toward you. Can't you see him waiting for your thanksgiving? The Bible is filled with descriptions of worshipful visions of God and profound encounters with Jesus or the Spirit, and all of these can provide you with fruitful material for your prayers.

The more vividly you picture these scenes as you read them, the more helpful they will prove to your prayer. Why not try to use your imagination to embrace the entire experience—the setting, the events and the emotions—not just the words on the page?

You may find it helpful as you read to try to identify with the person or people experiencing God. In praying the passage from Isaiah, for example, read it slowly a few times. Picture in your mind what it might have been like for Isaiah to experience God in this way. Allow the images in the text to trigger similar images in your mind, images of majesty, power, supremacy and repentance. Meditate on God's character as this Scripture reveals it and allow yourself to respond to God as he reveals himself through the passage. You might then find yourself bowing in prayer, declaring to God how awesome he really is. Don't be too concerned with words and formulas. Rather, let the experience of the passage inspire your own experience of God, who is the same today as in Isaiah's day.

One of the most prominent elements of worship and praise

you will discover as you read Scriptures that teach about or describe them is that worship and praise are to be done. The very language for *worship* and *praise* in the Scriptures demonstrates just how much the human body is involved. The apostle Paul says, "I *bow* my knees before the Father" (Ephesians 3:14). When John saw a glimpse of Christ in his heavenly attire, he recounts, "I *fell* at his feet as though dead" (Revelation 1:17). Psalm 147:1 declares, "How good it is to *sing* praises to our God." The Scriptures encourage us to kneel, bow, lift our hands, sing, shout, dance and much more—all in expression of worship and praise to God.

There is something significant about getting physical in worship. Posture, gestures and actions both reflect and cultivate attitudes toward God in worship, just as they affect attitudes to all of life. Why not try praying the Scriptures by *doing* what they suggest? Go ahead—lift your hands to the Lord in praise, bow down before the Almighty, give a joyous shout to the Lord—a real shout! You may feel awkward in the beginning (and you may need some privacy to feel comfortable), but as you explore putting your body into worship, you will soon find yourself getting in touch with the heart of the attitude of worship and praise in ways you have never experienced.

The prayers and the pictures of worship and thanksgiving draw our minds and hearts into prayer that resembles the worship of inspired Scripture. We are enriched, and God receives great glory. LIST C offers a listing of these types of prayers and pictures found in the Old and New Testaments. To make it easy to find an appropriate passage, they are arranged by type (picture of worship, thanksgiving prayers, etc.) and by location in the Bible.

5

BIBLICAL
MEDITATION
·······································

*"THY KINGDOM COME,
THY WILL BE DONE."*

My favorite image of meditation is a cow chewing its cud. The cow first bites off some grass, chews it up and swallows it. Then the cow regurgitates, allowing the food to come back up to be rechewed and reswallowed, again and again, until all the nutrients are absorbed.

We act in the same way when we meditate. We bite off a piece of a Scripture or a thought about God. We chew it up, thinking about it. And then we swallow it, allowing it to penetrate our hearts. But we are nourished even more when we allow a passage or thought to come back up in our minds again and again, slowly letting all the nutrients make their way into the deepest parts of our being.

This is the primary distinction between meditation and other forms of prayer: we often use the term *prayer* to describe talking *to* God, whereas we use the word *meditation* to describe the repeated placement of our attention on thoughts *about* God. Meditation unites reason, imagination and feeling during a period of being present with God. When we meditate, we think about God, we picture things of God, and we experience feelings toward God.

In Psalm 77:12 the psalmist, afraid and sad because he doesn't presently experience the Lord's mighty power, declares, "I will meditate on all your work, and muse on your mighty deeds." He decides that it would be good to reflect on God's mighty deeds, to remind himself again of who God is. How does the psalmist do this? He recalls to his mind God's landmark work in the history of Israel, the parting of the Red Sea and Israel's crossing to safety:

> When the waters saw you, O God,
>   when the waters saw you, they were afraid,
>   the very deep trembled.
> The clouds poured out water;
>   the skies thundered;
>   your arrows flashed on every side.
> The crash of your thunder was in the whirlwind;
>   your lightnings lit up the world;
>   the earth trembled and shook.
> Your way was through the sea,
>   your path, through the mighty waters;
>   yet your footprints were unseen.
> You led your people like a flock
>   by the hand of Moses and Aaron. (Psalm 77:16-20)

Now the written record of this parting of the Red Sea in Exodus 14 says nothing about thunder and lightning or earthquakes. Neither does it discuss the waters being afraid or trembling. It is likely that the psalmist is simply imagining what it might have been like. He thinks about the event, pictures it in his mind and feels what it must have felt like to be one of the people crossing that great sea, walking on dry land. And he comes away with a renewed confidence: "Your way, O God, is holy. What god is great as our God?" (Psalm 77:13).

Just like the writer of Psalm 77, believers of every generation have found it enriching to meditate on God's character and works by recalling events or themes in Scripture and letting themselves be drawn into them. Puritan author Richard Baxter, writing about meditation on God's holy angels and the celestial kingdom, encourages the believer to "get the liveliest picture of them in thy mind that thou possibly canst by contemplating the scriptural account of them till thou canst say, 'Methinks I see a glimpse of glory! Methinks I hear the shouts of praise, and even stand by Abraham and David and Peter and Paul and other triumphant souls!' " Likewise, the early Puritan father Lewis Bayly, in his classic work *The Practice of Piety*, asserts that we know God best "when from the true and lively sense of God's attributes, there is bred in a man's heart a love, awe and confidence in God."

For centuries Christians have cultivated a vivid and lively sense of the passages of the Scriptures. It is precisely this combination of imagination and emotion that is so helpful for our use in meditating on the events and themes of the Bible. How thrilling it is to enter into the Scriptures and to perceive God with our whole heart and mind and soul! As we bring reason, imagination and feeling to our meditation, we encourage wholehearted surrender to our King.

I will review two simple methods for meditating on God using the Scriptures. *Theological meditation* reflects on the nature of God and on the great themes of the faith. *Gospel meditation* reflects on the events in Jesus' life as recorded in the Gospels.

Theological Meditation

Choosing the topic and passages. Theological meditation begins when you pick a great theme or doctrine and find passages that discuss it. LIST D includes the primary Christian themes or doctrines and cites a few texts appropriate to each for meditation. You can also find Scriptures by using Bible appendices, a concordance, a Bible dictionary or a theology textbook.

If you choose the cross of Christ as a theme, for example, you can look up key words like *cross* or *death* and briefly read the verses listed to see which passages would be appropriate for meditation. You might pick five or six, such as the following: Luke 23:26-56 (the crucifixion), Luke 14:27 (carrying the cross), Romans 5:6-11 (Christ died for sinners), Philippians 2:1-11 (being of the same mind as Christ) and Colossians 2:13-15 (Christ is victorious on the cross).

Opening in prayer and reading the Scripture. Begin meditation with a brief prayer asking God to reveal himself more deeply. In this example you might ask God to enlighten your mind and heart to the reality and the significance of Christ's death on the cross, then read the passages you have chosen. Read them slowly, allowing your mind to move from text (what the passage says) to context (what it meant at the time of its writing and initial reading) and to life (what it means to your personal situation).

Feeling and reflecting on truths of Scripture. Just sit with each passage for a while. Allow the depth of its truths to work into your soul. You may have heard these truths many times before but never have allowed them to sink into the deeper parts of your being. Theological meditation accomplishes this. It provides the means by which plain words become living truth. Allow your heart to be stirred, moved and touched by the truth of the Scriptures.

Move from passage to passage as you find nourishment for your soul. If you are meditating on the cross, you might start by reading and reflecting on the description of Christ's crucifixion in Luke. You may get a good feel for the reality of Jesus' death on this day of meditation, but the passage may not "send you"—no great revelation comes. If so, move on to passages about carrying your cross and following Jesus' example.

The significance of the cross as an example for living might touch you deeply. Stay with thoughts of "cross living," feeling how far you are from Jesus' standard. Then turn to Romans and see how the Lord has brought reconciliation between you and the Father through the cross. Hallelujah! Even though you are far from the standard, you are not far from God. The Lord has come close to you through the cross. Turning to Colossians, you will find that the powers bringing destruction to your life have been conquered through the cross.

One insight feeds another, and you begin to delight in the knowledge that you can gain power for cross living, thanks to the victory won by Christ. The significance of the cross is made alive to you as you slowly turn the passages over in your mind. As you spend time reading, feeling and reflecting on these passages one by one, each brings up new material for meditation, and your understanding of the theme expands in prayer until at times your sight of the Lord may become nearly overwhelming.

I have used a form of this method with great benefit as a supplement to my time of biblical study. More than once when I have been bothered by an especially difficult problem of the Christian faith, I have applied this method of study and meditation to find my way out. One such problem during my college days was the subject of economic issues. How was I to think about issues of justice in the world? Was I to pursue earthly riches as the blessings of the Lord, or was I to seek simplicity of life, shunning worldly wealth? What should be my response to the plight of the poor in the world, to the plight of the poor in my neighborhood? How was I to balance this concern with interests in evangelism?

I attacked this problem through a program of study. I got out my concordance and looked up passage after passage that talked about money, wealth, poverty, riches, oppression and more. Periodically, however, I would lay the books aside and spend time reflecting on the Scriptures that I was reading, not as a student of theology but as a student of *God*. In these times I would ask, "Lord, what do these passages, these themes mean to our society? to me? How can my life glorify you in my approach to issues of money?" I imagined the possibilities. I considered the costs. I repented and prayed for grace. In the end the Lord has his way.

The combination of study and prayer over these Scriptures

led me not only to answers for theological questions, but also to the beginnings of a view of the heart of God, and eventually to life decisions that would shape the course of my journey with God and with others. I cannot recommend enough the practice of theological meditation.

Gospel Meditation

Ignatius of Loyola was a soldier in the early sixteenth century. It was the age of chivalry in Spain, and Ignatius was passionate for the taste of battle. One day he got his chance in a skirmish over the control of a nearby city. When others fled, he remained and fought. But Ignatius's fighting ended abruptly when the enemy shot a cannonball that passed between his legs, shattering one and damaging the other.

Ignatius was forced to lie in bed for recuperation. He had in the home where he stayed nothing to read but a book on the life of Jesus and a book on the history of the saints. The bedridden soldier found himself spending time imagining the stories in the books he read. He pictured Christ interacting with his disciples, traveling from city to city, healing and preaching. He heard the confessions of the saints, boldly proclaiming Christ as they were ridiculed or martyred for their faith. Ignatius began to imagine himself undertaking gospel exploits for the kingdom of Christ. He imagined himself preaching; he heard Christ calling him to follow. He saw Christ dying on the cross for him.

By the time he had healed, Ignatius of Loyola was a changed man. His passion for personal glory was transformed into a fervent desire for the glory of Christ. He became the founder of the Society of Jesus, a religious order that has established schools and missions all over the world. His *Spiritual Exercises* has become a classic manual of prayer, especially of Gospel meditation. Let's follow Ignatius's example of Gospel meditation.

Choosing a story. To practice Gospel meditation, pick a story from Matthew, Mark, Luke or John. LIST E offers a number of Gospel stories that illustrate various aspects of God's character. They are arranged by meditation theme and by their location in the various Gospels.

Opening in prayer. Take a minute to pray, and ask God to teach you, protect you and guide you in your meditation. Remember: the Lord, whose life is recorded in the Gospels, lives in you today, and the Holy Spirit who inspired the Scripture inspires you today.

Reading the passage. Next read the passage you've chosen. Read it a few times if necessary to get a sense of the setting and the development of the story. If you have a question ("I wonder what roofs were like in those days"), briefly consult a Bible dictionary. You may wish to do this before beginning, or you can wait until afterward (you can always do the meditation again with the newly acquired information). Your goal at this stage is to develop a basic mental image of the setting where the events took place.

Picturing the scene. Now allow the setting of the passage to appear before you as if you were watching a movie, or better, as if you were *there*. Allow your mind to get an imaginative grasp of what would be sensed. If you were meditating on a story of Jesus' ministry in a village by the Sea of Galilee, you would want to see the expressions on people's faces as they relate to Jesus. You would hear the comments of the bystanders, the disciples, the religious leaders. Smell the market-place, the sea breezes; touch the Savior's garment or the leper; drink from the cup that is passed. Allow your whole person to identify with the story.

Participating in the story. You may find that you particularly identify with one person in the story. This is perfectly all right. In fact, stories—even biblical stories—are written to encourage a variety of people to identify with the characters and to be drawn into the story. If it seems appropriate, imagine you are one of the people in the story. Become that person. Perhaps you are the woman who longs to touch Jesus' garment and be healed. Perhaps you are Peter, who rashly cuts off the guard's ear when Jesus is threatened. Perhaps you are in the crowd, watching nervously as Jesus is nailed to the cross. Allow your mind to play as you interact with the passage. You may even wish to imagine a hypothetical conversation with another person in the story, even with Christ. Because the Lord who lived the story is alive today, this conversation can become a form of prayer.

Evaluating and recording the experience. As you close your time of meditation, it is helpful to review and summarize the experiences and issues that come up. You could even record your experiences of meditation in a journal for review later. Did your mind stay close to the general plot and teaching of the passage, or did it wander far from the intended message of the passage? What do you now more clearly understand about yourself or God? Into what new steps of faith might God be inviting you?

This method need not be restricted to the Gospels. It is a wonderful method to glean inspiration from any of the stories of Scripture. Like Ignatius, we all need heroes in our lives. You can use meditation like this to stimulate your desire to imitate the leadership of Moses, the courage of Esther, the humility of Old Testament Joseph, the ministry of Priscilla. Find those examples of godly character in Scripture that excite you and spend some time meditating on their stories, allowing your own life to be drawn into imitation of these heroes of the faith.

Theological and Gospel meditation also enable us to come into contact with our Lord more deeply. By engaging ourselves fully with the themes and stories of the Bible, we can stimulate our appreciation for the reign of God and cultivate a passion to see his kingdom come and his will be done.

6

PETITION & INTERCESSION
Praying for Our Needs

....

"GIVE US THIS DAY OUR DAILY BREAD."

Lord, help me!"

"And God bless Mommy and Daddy and Grandma and everybody."

We learn petition and intercession as children. Children are used to asking for what they need. There is nothing more spontaneous than a cry for help. But when directed toward God, such a cry becomes a form of prayer. Our cries for help, our mundane requests, our pleas on behalf of another—these are all petitions or intercessions. A *petition* is simply a request for ourselves or others. *Intercession* is prayer on behalf of others.

We do not believe in a God who is aloof or unconcerned about our lives. God numbers the very hairs on our head (Matthew 10:30). He is acquainted with all our ways (Psalm

139:3). Nothing can separate us from "the love of God in Jesus Christ our Lord" (Romans 8:39). The concerns and the details of our lives are the concerns of the compassionate Savior. Scripture invites us to bring our concerns and requests to God, so we don't need to "worry about anything, but in everything by prayer and supplication with thanksgiving let [our] requests be made known to God" (Philippians 4:6).

The stories of God's answers to prayer are familiar to us. Many have lifted up a petition in a time of need and seen God work mighty deeds to answer the request. Many saints have made intercession a significant part of their ministry, working miracles by their prayers for others. In answer to the requests of his people God has comforted the sorrowful, healed the sick and caused the hardhearted to receive the gospel.

Despite these inspiring stories, it is often difficult for us to move beyond "Lord, help me!" and "God bless Mommy and Daddy" to a sense of confidence and effectiveness in our petitions and intercessions. Sometimes we don't ask God for things because we are afraid of being disappointed or ignored. But the problem is not always as difficult as wrestling with the complexities of unanswered prayer (I will address this topic in chapter ten). Often we just don't know *what* to pray, so we don't pray. This is where the practice of praying the Scriptures enters.

How to Practice Petition and Intercession

Here are a few methods that will help you explore beyond the simple petitions you may have learned as a child.

Studying the petitions. As I have said, many passages of

Scripture are prayers themselves. By examining the *content* of the scriptural requests we learn what kinds of things the inspired authors of Scripture asked for in their petitions and intercessions. By examining the *form* of these prayers we learn something of how to make requests to God. We see what attitudes these authors held, how they pleaded their cases, what they felt and how they understood God's relationship to their problems. From all of this we get a feel for how we might pray to God about our own concerns.

Speaking the prayers. In praying the Scriptures we do not merely examine the prayers of the Bible, we also speak them ourselves: we put them into our own words, making our concerns and requests fit the form and content of the biblical prayers.

Let's say you know you are facing a stressful month. Obligations to family, friends, work and church are converging upon you. In a time like this you might turn to the petition in Isaiah 26:7-9:

> The way of the righteous is level;
> O Just One, you make smooth the path of the righteous.
> In the path of your judgments,
> O LORD, we wait for you;
> your name and your renown
> are the soul's desire.
> My soul yearns for you in the night,
> my spirit within me earnestly seeks you.

Notice how Isaiah looks toward the "smooth" path of the righteous. See how he waits for the intervention of God and how his possession of the person of God appears to be the foremost aim of this prayer. The themes (waiting, trust, pleading) and the feelings (longing, seeking) will then instruct your own prayer to God. You might lift up your own prayer to God in a form similar to that of Isaiah's prayer:

> *Lord, I thought your way was the best way.*
> *This month it sure doesn't feel like it.*
> *I can't straighten things out, Lord, so I wait for you.*
> *I will simply follow the path of obedience*
>   *to what you have commanded me.*
> *And I will wait for you to do the rest.*
> *All I really want in the midst of this mess is you, Lord Jesus.*
> *More than anything I yearn to know your presence close*
>   *to me*
>   *and to be close to you*
> *in every situation that confronts me.*

You can use other biblical prayers in a similar manner. One of Paul's prayers for the saints, recorded in his letters, might give words and feeling to your prayers for loved ones. Prayers written for special ceremonies, for the healing of others and for the effectiveness of ministry also help to express in prayer what you feel.

The words of those coming to Jesus can also give voice to your own cry. Many people came to him, pleading on behalf of their needs or those of a loved one. I have found it helpful to identify with these people, using their pleas to express my own heart to Jesus. These prayers may be quite brief, but they are right to the point, and they often communicate my "Help, Lord!" sentiments exactly.

Repeating a petition. Another approach is to choose a phrase of petition and repeat it. The phrase "Lord Jesus Christ, have mercy on me, a sinner" is based on the prayer of the tax collector in Luke 18:13. For centuries Christians in Eastern Europe have recited this "Jesus Prayer" as a means of praying constantly throughout the day.

One delightful story of this practice recounts the wanderings of an anonymous Russian pilgrim on his journeys through Russia and Siberia. As the story begins, the pilgrim encounters a Christian holy man who encourages him to practice repeating the Jesus Prayer throughout the day. The mentor dies, and the pilgrim begins his journey with two rubles, a bag of dried bread and the lessons learned of the Jesus Prayer. The pilgrim says of this departure, "Again I started off on my wanderings. But now I did not walk along as before, filled with care. The calling upon the name of Jesus Christ gladdened my way. Everybody was kind to me. It was as though everyone loved me." Like the pilgrim in the story, many of us can attest to the benefits of constantly bringing our burdens to the Lord in prayer.

How to Use Meditation When Petitioning

One way of praying the Scriptures fits somewhere in the border between biblical meditation and petition/intercession. I call it the *seeing-as* method. In petition/intercession your focus is primarily on your concern, and that concern is expressed *through* the Scripture in prayer. In biblical meditation your focus develops from the passage of Scripture meditation. In the seeing-as method you move from Scripture to life and back, as text and life come together meditatively. You can start either with a specific passage or theme of meditation or with a specific situation in life. In either case both are used. Move back and forth in your mind, reflecting on Scripture, on life, on Scripture, on life, until you *see* your life *as* an embodiment of the theme or text of meditation.

Let's say that you have a difficult personal decision to make at work. You have an opportunity to be promoted in the company, but this promotion would necessitate leaving out the tasks you enjoy most on the job. It would require more training and more responsibility, and it would potentially affect your family life and social relationships.

You have been spending some time in petition for guidance in this request. The only direction you have sensed is a feeling that it's time to move on and a concern that you serve the needs of your family. You decide to *see* this promotion *as* an expression of Jesus' washing the feet of his disciples, since that story speaks of humble service.

You might begin, then, by spending some time with the story in Gospel meditation, as described in the previous chapter. You might play the part of one of the disciples, allowing yourself to be washed by Jesus. How do you react to his service to you? Then return to your present situation. Imagine yourself in each of the options laid before you. Then try to *see* yourself *as* an expression of this story. In what ways might you become a servant of others as the passage indicates? How do you see yourself acting? Ideas might come to mind as you picture each option in light of your biblical meditation. (It may help to have a prayer of petition running through your mind as you reflect: "Make me a servant, Lord, I pray.") Perhaps you will see possibilities for appropriate service in both options. You could even merge the stories together and see Jesus in your workplace. What would he do if he were you?

In this way you go back and forth between story and life until you are satisfied that you have expressed and heard everything that was needed at this time. This method of praying the Scriptures will not answer all your life questions, but it is helpful at times to try to *see* your life or that of another *as* an expression of Christ or a theme of Scripture.

By reading the petitions and intercessions of the Bible we can get a sense of their dominant themes. By studying these prayers we can understand them in their original context and see what they show us about the relationship between God and his people. By personally identifying with the authors in their written requests, we can feel their heart for prayer. But most importantly, by praying them in our own words, for ourselves and for others, we can see the Lord act on our behalf. Our relationship with God will mature, and we will gain the confidence that "if we ask anything according to his will, he hears us. And if we know that he hears us in whatever we ask, we know that we have obtained the requests made of him" (1 John 5:14-15).

LIST F, "Praying for Personal and Corporate Needs," is a collection of passages that will help you to find words for your requests, and to get a feel for the prayers and pray-ers of the Scriptures. Nearly all of these passages are petitions or intercessions themselves, although a few mention but do not present the prayer. I have arranged them into categories that reflect both the types of prayer as they are found in the Scriptures and as you might have need of them.

7

REVIVAL PRAYER & PRAYING THE PROMISES OF SCRIPTURE

....

"ON EARTH AS IT IS IN HEAVEN."

Sometimes prayer arises from our hearts like the flow of a mighty geyser. Through reading a passage of Scripture, hearing a sermon or spending time in prayer, we come face to face with the living God. It is *God's* concerns and *God's* intentions that move our prayer. We feel the burden of the Lord, we understand the promises of Christ's kingdom, we see our own pitiful condition—and these drive us to intercession, petition and confession. I call praying in this manner for the progress of God's kingdom *revival prayer*.

Revival Prayer

Revival prayer is a form of petition and intercession. In revival prayer we make requests to God. But these requests are not of the "Give us this day our daily bread" type. In revival prayer requests do not arise from our sense of personal need; they are fueled by something that might best be described as a vision of God's heart. Revival prayer is also similar to a meditation on the kingdom of God. Yet it is not so much an expression of personal surrender to the King, but rather a passionate pleading for the life, or the rule, of the King to be established in individuals or groups where his absence is keenly felt.

Rees Howells knew this kind of prayer. Shortly after he had dedicated his life fully to the Lord during the Welsh revival of 1904, Rees Howells was moved to voice prayers that appeared as burdens from God's heart to his. The first prayer was for the town drunk, Will Battery. Howells's biography relates, "It was for this man that Mr. Howells, to his own surprise, found the Holy Ghost travailing through him." And eventually, in part through Rees Howells's fervent prayer and compassionate action, this man was brought to Christ. Soon after this man's conversion, Howells felt a similar burden from the Lord to see the conversion of a nearby village that had no Christians. Again the Spirit of Christ moved through prayer and compassionate action to reach the lost—an entire village.

Much later in life Howells and his wife moved to Gazaland, Africa. The Howellses and two other missionaries met each Thursday to read the Bible and pray for revival in their area. Gazaland had never experienced a move of God, but on Sunday, October 10, 1915, revival came. A young girl, Kufase, came to the meeting after fasting for three days under a conviction that she was not ready for the Lord's return. "As she prayed," Howells's own account records, "she broke down crying, and within five minutes the whole congregation were on their faces crying to God. Like thunder and lightning the power came down. We had two revival meetings every day for fifteen months without a single break, and meetings all day on Fridays. Hundreds were converted."

Fervent prayer for the revival of believers, fueled by a heartfelt sense of God's heart for his people, is found throughout Scripture. A number of the psalmists expressed revival prayer when making requests to God. Their deep sense of chosenness, inherited through centuries of remembered promises, together with their keen awareness of the miseries of failure and exile, found expression in impassioned prayers asking God to restore his people once again. Thus Asaph prays in Psalm 74:1-3, 22:

> O God, why do you cast us off forever?
> > Why does your anger smoke against the sheep of your
> > > pasture?
> Remember your congregation, which you acquired long
> > ago,
> > which you redeemed to be the tribe of your heritage.
> > Remember Mount Zion, where you came to dwell.
> Direct your steps to the perpetual ruins;
> > the enemy has destroyed everything in the sanctuary. . . .
> Rise up, O God, plead your cause.

Revival prayer is especially common in the literature of the prophets, who deeply felt both the truth of Israel's election as God's kingdom and the lack of his reign over Israel in practice. Again and again, the prophets cried out to God for the restoration of the Spirit's promised work in the Spirit's promised people. These Scripture prayers make especially good models for our own prayers for the renewal of the church and the revival of God's purposes on earth in general.

The need for the renewal of God's power and rule among his people is as great today as it was centuries ago. Let's examine Jeremiah's prayer in Jeremiah 14:7-9 to see how these prayers can guide you in your prayers for revival in your family, your church and your nation.

> Although our iniquities testify against us,
>> act, O LORD, for your name's sake;
> our apostasies indeed are many,
>> and we have sinned against you.
> O hope of Israel,
>> its savior in time of trouble,
> why should you be like a stranger in the land,
>> like a traveler turning aside for the night?
> Why should you be like someone confused,
>> like a mighty warrior who cannot give help?
> Yet you, O LORD, are in the midst of us,
>> and we are called by your name;
>> do not forsake us!

Notice how the themes of confession, complaint and request wind their way through the prayer. Notice how the prophet's sense of abandonment is expressed through metaphors and images ("like a stranger in the land," "like someone confused"). Yet always the honor of God's name, God's concerns and God's reputation drive the prayer. The form, themes and emotion of this prayer can be used as you pray for revival in your own setting. Following the pattern of Jeremiah 14:7-9 you might pray like this for a church struggling with division:

Lord, I know we don't deserve your grace;
  we have fought against each other without end.
But for the sake of your reputation, God, in this community,
  for those things that you want most,
  restore this church to unity.
Turn our hearts and minds to your works and will, Lord.
Why must we cry for so long about these things
  and not find an answer?
Have you left our church forever?
Surely, Lord, you desire that we show forth your glory
  by our words and our lives.
You have said that the gates of hell
  shall not prevail against the church.
We are at fault, Lord. But we still bear your name.
For the sake of your name have mercy on us,
  and restore this church again!

Prayers like the one in Jeremiah 14 prove very helpful in providing form and inspiration both for your private prayers for revival and for prayer in gatherings of believers who want to call on the Spirit to bring revival.

Praying the Promises of Scripture

The writers of biblical prayers, and especially those who wrote revival prayers, often remind God of his character, past deeds and promises. Jeremiah, for example, reminds God that he is the savior in times of trouble, and calls on him to act in a situation just as he claims he can (Jeremiah 14). Likewise, in Psalm 74, Asaph argues that Israel, *as God's inheritance*, should not be neglected. Similarly, in Psalm 89,

Ethan the Ezrahite recalls in his prayer the promises spoken by Nathan to David and asks that they be established. In the example of prayer for church unity above we remind the Lord of Jesus' promise that "the gates of hell shall not prevail against the church" (Matthew 16:18).

In personal prayer today we commonly use the promises of Scripture to shape the form and content of our requests to God. Christian bookstores and even grocery-store counters keep promise books on their shelves. It is exciting to see believers shaping their faith and prayers around the promises of God. Improper use of this practice, however, can lead to the misplacement of faith and painful disappointment. Here are a few suggestions to avoid these problems.

1. Let God's promises, in the context of God's plan, guide your prayers. It is a good idea to read the Scriptures widely and deeply to get a feel for the nature of God's plan of salvation as promised and revealed in the Bible. This will educate your prayers in a general sense. Wide and deep reading of the Scriptures can also be helpful in deciding whether a particular passage is an appropriate promise to use in praying for a particular situation. If a passage of Scripture inspires your faith, I would advise you to seek to understand the promise of that particular passage in light of the whole plan of God before claiming that promise for your own life.

2. Seek to understand the promises of Scripture in their proper biblical context. Ask, "Am I praying in light of what this Scripture intends to communicate? Have I understood it appropriately? Does it promise what I think it does?"

Suppose you are experiencing a dry time in your relationship with God. The warm tingles you felt in prayer as a new

Christian have faded, and now you just kind of slump down on a chair during devotions and feel bored. You might call upon God to bring back those first feelings, reminding Jesus of his promise, "I am with you always" (Matthew 28:20). But look again: does this passage promise perpetual warm feelings? No! It does, however, assure you of God's presence no matter how you may feel.

3. Bring personal faith to these promises. It was the *conviction* that Israel was the people of God that enabled the prophets to pray for restoration with such fervor in spite of being a forgotten remnant in Babylonian exile. Such promises are expressions of the very heart of God. Don't minimize their potential by ignoring them. Faith in God has great power, so allow your faith to be awakened by meditation on these promises.

I have been greatly encouraged in my prayers for friends moving toward faith in Christ by a statement about the Messiah made in Isaiah 42:3. As repeated in Matthew 12:20, it says that God "will not break a bruised reed or quench a smoldering wick." The wick mentioned is a bunch of flax gathered together to catch a spark or tiny glowing coal used to start a fire. When a spark makes contact with the flax, it begins to smolder or smoke. Anyone who has ever tried to start a fire without a match knows that this is a critical moment. Only gentle blowing will transform the wick from a smolder to a true burn. Careful attention must be given not to blow too hard, or the wick will go out.

This metaphor gives a picture-promise of God's heart for us. God wants, even for the slightest indication of life, not to quench but to awaken life. I think of a friend who is young and weak in the Lord. She falls and stumbles in her walk so often. I remind God of this promise, this picture of God's character, and pray with confidence, "Blow her into flame, Jesus. If there is one spark of real faith in her, some measure of smoke, don't quench it. Lord, bring the fire of your Spirit into her life."

4. *Attune personal desires to God's desires when praying the promises of Scripture.* Jesus said, "If God so clothes the grass of the field, which is alive today and tomorrow is thrown into the oven, will he not much more clothe you?" (Matthew 6:30). But this does not mean that God is obliged to provide us with fashionable luxuries. James writes, "You ask and do not receive, because you ask wrongly, in order to spend what you get on your pleasures " (James 4:3). It would be an affront to God if we were to misapply his promises to our own desires.

5. *Don't expect God's promises to be a recipe for answered prayer.* By using the promises of God in your prayers you are reflecting God's own heart and concerns back to himself, not manufacturing a magic formula that will guarantee results. Even in prayer that recalls God's promises you are addressing the sovereign Lord. As we shall see in chapter ten, sometimes our most sincere prayers go unanswered. Picture yourself as a peasant pleading before the throne of a mighty king. You speak to the king about his wonderful character, of his promises. You make your case passionately and reasonably. But the king is still the king.

6. *Allow the texts that speak of God's promises and the context of life to interact.* Wait to claim a promise until you have a well-informed, heartfelt connection with a passage for your life or the life of others. A good indication of this readiness is when you have a sense through prayerful reading of the

Scriptures that *this* promise is for *this* time. Sometimes this happens as a Scripture works its way into your soul and begins to speak through your prayers, as in the example of the smoldering wick. At other times it comes as you hold a concern in prayer and a passage arises that fits the need. You may wish to use the *seeing-as* method, mentioned in chapter six, of bringing life and text together.

7. *Keep the prophetic and kingdom context of the promises in the forefront of your prayers.* This is especially important as you recite God's promises back to him. As much as possible, allow your prayers to be driven by God's concerns and plans more than your personal desires. In the sample rewording of Jeremiah 14 at the beginning of this chapter, you told the Lord, "You have said that the gates of hell shall not prevail against the church." Your concern here was the fulfillment of God's concerns, stated in the promise, which you identified as your own. In the same way you can take other of the Lord's own concerns back to him, calling on God to fulfill what *he* desires in the practical realities of your life.

Petitions and intercessions that come from a deep sense of the need for revival and that flow from a vision of God's plan and promises can be some of your most powerful prayers. By reading and meditating on the prayers for revival in the Scriptures and on the plan and the promises of God, you can cultivate faith for the concerns of God. By identifying with God's concerns revealed in Scripture you can begin to form your prayers around the matters that are closest to the heart of God. Finally, by praying these Scriptures you can voice these concerns and move mountains.

LIST G, "Prayers for Mercy and Revival," notes revival prayers from Scripture which can be helpful models for your own prayer. LIST H, "A Few Promises to Use in Prayer," offers some classic promises of Scripture on various themes.

8

CONFESSION & SELF-EXAMINATION

....

*"AND FORGIVE US OUR DEBTS,
AS WE FORGIVE OUR DEBTORS."*

God's word to us is "Be holy as I am holy." And the Bible is filled with specific commands that make clear what this holiness is to look like in our daily lives. But again and again we find ourselves falling short of God's standard of holiness. Our hearts stray, our minds wander, and time after time we find ourselves coming to God like a schoolboy facing his mother after hitting his baseball through the window—again.

Praying the Confessions of Scripture
The promise of Scripture is that "if we confess our sin, he who is faithful and just will forgive us our sins and cleanse us from all unrighteousness" (1 John 1:9). In previous chapters we have seen that we can use Scripture as a model for our confession. Many passages of Scripture are confessions of personal or corporate sins, especially in the Psalms and in the

prophets' writings. David's cry of confession in Psalm 51:1-4 says,

> Have mercy on me, O God,
>   according to your steadfast love;
> according to your abundant mercy
>   blot out my transgressions.
> Wash me thoroughly from my iniquity,
>   and cleanse me from my sin.
> For I know my transgressions,
>   and my sin is ever before me.
> Against you, you alone, have I sinned,
>   and done what is evil in your sight,
> so that you are justified in your sentence
>   and blameless when you pass judgment.

You can easily make this psalm your own simply by adding to it the specifics of your life situation. If you want to confess that you have lied to your family, you might reword the psalm like this:

> *O Lord, please forgive me.*
>   *Have mercy on me and don't harm me.*
> *Don't consider me according to my failures.*
> *I feel dirty for what I've done, Lord.*
>   *Please take my guilt away.*
> *I know I have done wrong.*
>   *I lied to my wife and children.*
> *I tried to cover up my hurt by more lies, and I said*
>   *many things that weren't true.*
> *Every time I go to bed this sin haunts me.*

Now I'm telling you that I apologize.
I've hurt you more than anybody,
  for it is a slap in your face when I resort to lying.
When I lie, I am saying that I don't trust you.
  It's really you I have sinned against.
And you would be right to punish me any way you please.
  I deserve it.

Scriptural prayers of this type are listed in chapter three and in LIST G, "Prayers for Mercy and Revival."

Beyond Confession to Self-Examination

One great quality I have discovered about the Scriptures is their power to help me move beyond confession to transformation. Paul exhorts believers, "Put off your old nature which belongs to your former manner of life and is corrupt through deceitful lusts, and be renewed in the spirit of your minds, and put on the new nature, created after the likeness of God in true righteousness and holiness" (Ephesians 4:22-24 RSV). Creative, prayerful meditation on your life in the light of the Scriptures can be a marvelous tool for this "putting off" and "putting on." It can help make you more deeply aware of your own particular sinful tendencies. In so doing, it helps you understand just why you tend to sin the way you do. A prayerful application of the Scriptures to your life can cultivate the reordering of belief systems and emotional patterns that hinder you from walking in "true righteousness and holiness." This meditative prayer of confession and re-formation is often called the *prayer of examen* or *self-examination*.

Self-examination is simply the act of prayerfully thinking over the events of your day. The eighteenth-century Anglican William Law writes of this practice: "This examination of ourselves every evening is, therefore, to be considered as something that is as necessary as a daily confession and repentance of our sins. Daily repentance has very little significance and loses all its chief benefit, unless it be a particular confession and repentance of the sins of that day."

A variety of techniques for self-examination have been developed in the history of the church. Saint Ignatius of Loyola (1491-1556), founder of the Jesuits, suggests choosing particular sins to address. After making a formal commitment to obedience when we wake up, we then think about how we have done regarding the sin in question at noon and in the evening. Jeremy Taylor (1613-1667), author of *Rules and Exercises of Holy Living*, encourages a more general review of the day, confessing what was bad and giving thanks for what was good.

The four techniques for self-examination presented here emphasize the Scriptures as a model and inspiration for the prayerful consideration of our lives. These methods focus on noticing the presence of sinful patterns, recognizing the nature of those patterns, applying truth to them and cultivating the practice of righteousness.

Noticing the Presence of Sin

At one period in my life I was keenly aware of a number of sinful habits that God wanted to root out of me. I would often come to my end-of-the-day prayer of self-examination only to discover how far I was from righteous living. Some of these sinful patterns were so subtle and so intertwined with my personality that I hardly noticed them. I made up lists of very specific rules: personal dos and don'ts. Sometimes these rules helped. Sometimes they just stirred my rebellion even more, or they fostered a kind of pharisaic legalism (one of the very sins God wanted removed).

During this same period I was reading in the epistles and found several places where the writers warned against the same sinful patterns I was fighting. I remember realizing that *here* were the rules I was looking for. These passages of Scripture were not overly specific like my lists were. Nonetheless, they were bold and to the point. I made a list of the ones that addressed my sinful patterns, and then I established a habit of meditating on them, asking the Lord each night to show me where I had fallen. I would ask, "Have I 'thought more highly of myself than I ought' today?" (Romans 12:3). "Have I 'shunned youthful lusts' today?" (2 Timothy 2:22). "Have I been 'devoted to prayer' today?" (Colossians 4:2). If during my meditation I identified where I had fallen astray, I confessed my sin and determined to get back on the path. Likewise, if while I was reading my passages and praying, I noticed a moment in my day where God was very present and I had gained a victory, I praised God for it.

At times this method led to unhealthy introspection and self-condemnation. When I spent too much thought on myself and not enough on God, prayerful self-examination became scrupulous self-analysis or rational planning for change. However, as long as I honestly approached those problem areas and viewed the time as *prayer before God,* my times of measuring myself against the Scriptures served to point out my failures and successes more clearly. And the more I practiced self-examination with the Scriptures, the more I began to notice my sin *just after* I sinned, and then *as* I sinned, then *before* I sinned. As I became aware of my sin sooner and sooner, I was better able to resist temptation and avoid the traps of sin.

If you want to begin examining yourself for the presence of sin, you will want to look for a few Scriptures that address the areas of your life about which God is speaking to you. If you don't know the areas of life or passages of Scripture that you want to use, try browsing through passages on holy Christian living. For example, read the epistles with a prayerful attitude, and ask the Holy Spirit to point out those passages God wants you to use for self-examination. Or just read through the Sermon on the Mount, looking for areas of your life that need reform. In LIST I, I have listed sections of the Bible that might be appropriate for this kind of reflection.

Having selected your Scriptures, set aside some time each evening or a free moment each day to prayerfully review the day. Weigh your thoughts, feelings and actions as they compare with the directives of some particular texts of Scripture. Ask yourself, "Did I fulfill this command or example to the best of my ability?" and "Was God's concern, as reflected in this passage, on my heart today?" Such questions serve to guide your time of self-examination. You may want to keep a journal to record the things that God brings to mind in your reflections. Allow time for confession, thanksgiving and evaluating future conduct.

Discerning the Nature of Sin

Some sins do not leave readily when we repent. Patterns or habits of life and thought can often have such a hold on us that even when we want to get rid of them, we can't. Noticing the sinful habits, the *presence* of sin, just makes us feel hopeless of ever changing. We hear the biblical exhortation to "lay aside every weight and the sin that clings so closely," but the problem is precisely that the sin clings *so closely:* we are so caught up and so easily and unconsciously distracted by a sinful pattern that it is seems impossible to lay aside the hindrance. I call these sins our "tough stains"—those that don't seem to come out with ordinary washing.

I have discovered a couple of Scripture-based self-examination exercises that are helpful in addressing the tough stains of our lives. These exercises bring us in touch with the history, worldview, triggers and factors that cause particular sins to rise in our lives. They focus on getting at the *nature* of the sin in our lives. In doing so they provide practical means of putting off the old nature and putting on the new (Ephesians 4:22-24).

Reflect on the history of the sin. In his *Spiritual Exercises* Ignatius of Loyola encourages people to reflect on their history of sin. In an adaption of his exercise you begin by reading and rereading the story of the first sin, found in Genesis 3. Get a sense of the story's place and events. Ask the Lord to increase your awareness of sin and to give you appropriate sorrow for it. Then imagine the story taking place before you, watching it happen as though peeking from behind a bush. Listen to the serpent offer the temptation. See Eve pick the fruit. Consider her thoughts. Hear God searching for Adam. Then you might place yourself in the roles of each of the characters—the serpent, Eve, Adam, God—identifying with their thoughts and feelings. How do Adam and Eve approach the temptation? What factors influence Adam and Eve to sin? How do they make the choice to sin? How do they behave when they sin? What are the consequences?

Then write out a history of your own sin, starting at the beginning with the particular sin in question. As in the previous step, note the beginning, movements, acts and consequences of this sin. What factors had even the slightest influence on you? How did you feel? Why did you incline toward sin at different times? What were you expecting to gain from this sinful pattern? Why were you expecting this? Leave no stone unturned, and be bold enough to confess everything. If others had a bad influence on you, admit your hurt and forgive them. You may be unconscious of aspects of your sin, so feel free to ask the Lord to show them to you. Be thorough but not morbidly introspective. It may take some time to accomplish this, and it may be wise to pursue this in dialogue with a trusted friend, a counselor or spiritual leader. This part of the exercise is similar to what recovery groups call a "thorough moral review."

Now go back to the Scriptures. Having a new grasp on the history of our sin, you may want to reflect on the character of sin as discussed elsewhere in the Scriptures (the book of Judges offers a general overview). You could do a theological meditation on sin as shown in chapter five, allowing the texts and your life to play back and forth in your mind in the context of prayer. Allow the Scriptures to speak to the deep parts of your life—your hopes, fears, disappointments and gut beliefs. Allow the truth of your life's patterns to rise up in prayerful meditation. Finally, allow the content of the time of prayer to be brought before the cross of Christ, where all of our sin and contrition have their final resting place. Through this practice you can glean valuable insights concerning sinful tendencies, insights that you can use to gain victory over them.

Reflecting on the stages and patterns of sin. Past experiences, habitual cycles of behavior, deeply held fears and compulsive acts all have played a part in forming us into who we are, for better or worse. These same factors also play a part in the present, preventing us from realizing freedom over sinful tendencies. Core beliefs, those things which we believe not merely with our lips and minds but with our hearts and gut reactions, also play their part in shaping our sinful tendencies.

Often tough stains develop through identifiable stages. Two Scripture passages in particular can be valuable for helping you to get a fuller understanding of the sin in your life. Paul and James both give accounts of the progression of human sin.

The Stages of Sin's Formation: Romans 1:18-32

Stage 1: Their "minds became darkened" (v. 21). We form false beliefs.

Stage 2: They "exchanged the truth for a lie" (v. 25). We hold to lies and act on them.

Stage 3: "God gave them up" (vv. 24, 28). We find ourselves powerless over a cycle of behavior.

Stage 4: They "deserve the due penalty for their error" (vv. 27, 32). We experience unpleasant consequences.

The Cycle of Sin's Effect: James 1:12-15

Stage 1: We are "lured and enticed by desires" (v. 14). We are preoccupied with sinful thoughts or feelings.

Stage 2: Desire "gives birth to sin" (v. 15). Our preoccupation leads to compulsive or habitual behavior.

Stage 3: Sin gives birth "to death" (v. 15). Our behavior results in destruction and despair.

These two passages can be used as models for deep meditation on your own personal patterns of sinfulness.

As you reflect on each stage of the progression, begin to identify those factors that affect your way of life. Acknowledge those factors that can and those that cannot be controlled. Physical factors, psychological factors and spiritual factors all will come into reflection.

Since anxiety or worry is a problem for many of us, I will use this as an example. If you struggle with a bondage to worry in your life and want to meditate on the stages in Romans, you might begin with the verse about "minds being darkened." You would identify elements of your *beliefs* about yourself, your situation and your God which are false (some of these beliefs are inherited unconsciously from your culture), and which underlie the anxiety and worry in your life. Then you would move to "exchanging the truth for a lie" and identify the subtle *lies* used to justify your worry. You would notice the excuses you use to permit your preoccupation with fearful thoughts, excuses that do not hold water, realizing just how false they are. Then you would look back on your own experience and notice the point when God gave you up to worry, when it became out of control and a habitual *cycle* was born, a pattern you could not break. Finally, you will see the ugly *consequences* of your worry—what you are really missing because of it. You then would examine the character of the judgment of God in your life, both in the actual present and the potential future.

Another common pattern of sin is that of sexual lust. If you want to address a bondage to sexual lust using prayerful meditation on the cycle given in James, you would begin with those "lures and enticements" to your desires. You would notice the various experiences that have habitually triggered lust in your life. You would identify the precise nature of your *preoccupation* with sexual thoughts (who, what, when, where, why, how) by recalling a number of occasions in your past. See how you have been lured away from the peace of God, and note where your escape routes could have been. Next, reflect on how these sexual enticements or preoccupations have "given birth to sin." Note those *compulsive behaviors* flowing from inappropriate desire which can clearly be identified as sinful thoughts or behaviors. Doing so makes you aware of the patterns of lust as a *habit* in your life. Finally, meditate on the "death" that this pattern brings into your life. Looking very carefully at the *destruction* that lust is bringing to you, you might *despair* of ever experiencing life.

You may want to write your reflections in a private journal and share them with a spiritual friend. During one season of self-examination I read my journal out loud to a friend periodically, who then prayed each time for my forgiveness and healing. I was grateful for those times of confession and self-examination.

Identifying our unique way of following the patterns of

sin outlined in the Scriptures given above and identifying our own personal reasons for this pattern help us greatly to identify the means and the strength for breaking the stronghold of these patterns in our lives. By praying scriptural confessions, by examining ourselves through the prayerful reading of Scripture and by working through the history and stages of our sin by means of biblical meditation, we come to see the darker corners of our lives the way God does. We see the hurt and the painfulness of our sin before the almighty God. We feel the tragedy of sin in our lives, in our communities and in the world at large. We also experience the deep forgiveness of God, who wipes away every tear. Thus, those weights and sins which are not so easy to lay aside can be understood in greater depth as we prayerfully look at their nature in the light of Scripture.

The Application of Truth to Sin

Knowing how to perceive the *presence* of sin through daily self-examination and having identified the *nature* of sin through in-depth biblical meditation, you are now ready to make an aggressive counterattack on sin through the meditative application of truth to your situation. The methods of biblical meditation I call *application of truth to sin* cultivate a wholehearted putting off of the old nature: We look at our life in light of the truth of Scripture and allow ourselves to be touched and moved, and thus by God's grace to be transformed in our habitual patterns of thought and action.

Take the struggle of battling with lust. What do the Scriptures say about sexual desire and respect for others? First, they say that to look on a woman (or man) with lust is to commit adultery in one's heart (Matthew 5:28). So take this passage at its word.

When you find yourself looking at another person or an image of another person and begin to lust or to fantasize, try taking the imagination one step further. Imagine what an adulterous relationship with this woman (or man) would truthfully be like. You might imagine the pain in your family or in the family of the other person—the destruction, the grief, the sorrow. Imagine the beautiful lives and families that would be destroyed. Imagine the cost to your self-image, your relationships with people and your relationship with God. All of these scenarios are the likely consequences of a core belief that treats others as objects. Imagining the truth of this passage of Scripture will bring God's approach to sin home to your heart.

Other passages of Scripture work in a similar manner for a variety of sinful patterns. Is your problem fear or worry? Read Matthew 6:25-34 and imagine the futile attempt to add hours to your life through concerted worry. Go ahead: try to worry yourself some more hours! Do you have a problem with inappropriate expression of anger? Meditate on Matthew 5:21-22 and imagine murdering someone with your words. Is gossip or backbiting a problem? You may want to study James 3:1-12 and imagine your words as sparks that burn and spread into a wildfire, destroying everyone around you.

When we take the truth of Scripture to its logical conclusions, we begin to see and feel how silly our sinful habits are. And as we do this prayerfully, God will begin to give suggestions for further action and transformation. This is one helpful way to begin to putting off the old nature.

Cultivation of the Practice of Righteousness

Finally, you can cultivate righteousness through the putting on of the new nature. Again, this can be done through the practice of biblical meditation. In these exercises you begin to imagine a life in harmony with the heart of God as revealed in the Scriptures.

Let's look at your confrontation with worry. Picture Jesus saying to you, as to Jairus when he discovered that his daughter was dead, "Do not fear, only believe" (Mark 5:36). You might try picturing yourself as "a bird of the air" (Matthew 6:25-34) and see how God truly cares for you. Allow the meditation on these passages to bring you into a sense of confidence and rest in God's care.

Similarly, in your cultivation of a chaste mind you may wish to read through the Gospel of Luke, stopping at every story where Jesus had a significant encounter with a woman (this exercise can be used with benefit by both men and women). You might want to try a Gospel meditation on those stories where Jesus interacted with women, to see how Jesus treated them. See him care for the widow of Nain's grief through the raising of her son. Hear him point out the woman who donated so little to the church offering. Plain as she was, Jesus expressly noticed her. Feel the difference between your own reaction to the sinful woman at Jesus' feet and Jesus' reaction. Allow yourself to become impressed at Jesus' kind and sensitive treatment of women. Repeated meditations will inspire you to emulate Jesus' attitude. You also might want to begin to treat others as sisters or brothers in your imagination, applying to your life the Scripture that says to treat younger women as sisters (1 Timothy 5:2). As in the chapter on petition, you learn to meditatively *see* your life *as* an expression of Scripture.

The exercises of aggressive putting off and putting on are especially helpful during the heat of the day. When you begin to feel a sinful thought or behavior arising, try picturing the devil as a roaring lion nearby (1 Peter 5:8). When depression begins to overwhelm you, call to mind the heavenly hope to which Christ has called you. When alcohol begins to draw you away, imagine yourself being "filled with the Spirit, singing songs and hymns and spiritual songs" (Ephesians 5:18-19). Again, as you consider the Scriptures in this manner, specific practical ideas will come to your mind, and you will be inspired to a new walk with God.

The Bible is full of metaphors that make the intentions and commands of Scripture more vivid to the reader. Take advantage of them! They were written for your inspiration, to feed your imagination and stimulate you to new life. Notice the crossroads where you are asked to choose between the impulse of sin and the impulse of the Spirit. As you recognize an impulse to sin, you may wish to symbolically "put off" or throw away the temptation with a slight toss of your hand. You could even run a short distance, "fleeing" from the temptation of the devil.

In confession, self-examination and the aggressive pursuit of transformation, the method of obedience to the Scriptures mentioned in chapter one becomes very important. Our aim in praying the Scriptures is not simply that we might remember the Scriptures, but that we might embody them. The saints of the desert in the early centuries of Christianity spent hours reading, reciting and meditating on the Scriptures alone and in small gatherings. They were famous for their holy lives. Was there a connection? I believe so. These men and women were convinced that the words of the Scripture must give birth to a life of Scripture. "Do what is written," Gerontius of the desert said. This is how we come to know the glories of the Christian life.

The Scriptures can become a powerful partner in our prayers of confession and prayers for transformation. By reading the Scriptures in a spirit of prayer we can recognize the presence of sin more easily. By praying the confessions found in Scripture we can give voice to our own confession of sin and receive the matchless forgiveness of God. By meditating on our lives in light of the Scriptures we can gain deep insight into the nature of sin. And by aggressively and prayerfully applying the truth of Scripture to our lives, we can, by the Spirit, take victorious steps forward toward putting off the old nature and putting on the new.

In LIST I, "Commandments and Scriptural Exhortations," I have listed some of the main sections of Scripture that speak of specific sins to put off and behaviors to pursue. Some portions of the Old Testament Law are best understood with help from a commentary or a well-informed friend or pastor. They are large portions of Scripture and are best used to identify areas in our life that the Lord desires to transform. We should read through the passages prayerfully to find our place of need, then pray through those specific passages regularly to note our progress.

9

DELIVERANCE
PRAYER
Praying the
"Enemy" Psalms

....

"AND LEAD US NOT INTO TEMPTATION,
BUT DELIVER US FROM EVIL."

I was beginning to get excited about this praying the Scriptures stuff. It was my second year of seminary, and I had learned much from praying the prayers of Paul, Moses, Hannah and others. I was ready to try the Psalms. Convinced that the psalms could serve as models for my own prayer life, I had decided to try praying through one every day. My goal was to place myself into the language, the mind and the heart of the person praying that psalm and to try to make it my own prayer to God.

I started out zealously identifying with the psalm that was before me each new morning. But before long I ran into psalms like these:

Rise up, O LORD!
  Deliver me, O my God!

For you strike all my enemies on the cheek;
   you break the teeth of the wicked. (Psalm 3:7)

You made my enemies turn their backs to me,
   and those who hated me I destroyed.
They cried for help, but there was no one to save them;
   they cried to the LORD, but he did not answer them.
I beat them fine, like dust before the wind;
   I cast them out like the mire of the streets. (Psalm 18:40-42)

These were not the nice prayers I was used to praying, and I found many more like them. They caught me by surprise. It wasn't that I didn't know how these psalm writers felt; I sometimes wanted to call down a similar prayer for this guy at work who got on my nerves. But I also remembered Jesus' statement that I should pray *for* my enemy (Matthew 5:43-47). In this way I came face to face with the question "How do I use these enemy psalms as models for my own prayer life?"

As I examined the texts more closely over the years, I discovered that in the enemy psalms we find excellent examples of what has become popularly known as *warfare praying*. Warfare praying, or what I call *deliverance prayer*, is the practice of praying against the influence of the enemies of God over an individual or a place. It is, in effect, a prayer for deliverance. To show the relationship between the enemy psalms and deliverance prayer I will address three questions in this chapter: Who is the enemy in the Old Testament? Who is the Christian's enemy? And how can Christians use the enemy psalms?

Who Is the Enemy in the Old Testament?

In the Old Testament the term *enemy* generally refers to

three distinct entities.

The political or personal enemy. David speaks in 1 Samuel 29:8 of going to fight against the enemies of the king, namely the Philistines. He cries to God in Psalm 27:12, "Do not give me up to the will of my adversaries, for false witnesses have risen against me." David was the king of God's chosen people, the Israelites. A threat to David's kingship was a threat to the nation, and therefore a threat to God's plan. David's personal and political enemies were God's enemies. Thus David can say of his enemies, "The wicked perish, and the enemies of the LORD are like the glory of the pastures; like smoke they vanish away" (Psalm 37:20). David's reign was the fulfillment of the covenant, the promise of God. In this case we see that *enemy* in the Old Testament can refer to personal and political enemies insofar as they are the enemies of God, a direct threat to God's plan of salvation.

The people of God themselves when they are immersed in sin. Under David's reign all the threats to God's promise appeared on the outside; the enemies were the other guys. But as time passed and God's people grew more and more corrupt, it became increasingly appropriate for them to say, "We have met the enemy, and he is us." The persistent sin of God's people was now the threat to God's promise. Thus the prophet Isaiah records that God says of Israel, 'Ah! I will pour out my wrath on my enemies, and avenge myself on my foes! I will turn my hand against *you*' " (Isaiah 1:24-25).

The supernatural enemy. As time passed, there arose among the people of God a growing consciousness of a third enemy, an evil supernatural being who guided events and deceived people. We call that being Satan or the devil. The devil is never explicitly referred to as the enemy in the Old Testament, although Job 1—2 suggests as much. But in later Jewish writings before the time of Christ, he is often called an enemy. Satan is the one who deceives and accuses people, leading them away from God and threatening the fulfillment of God's promises.

So as we read the Old Testament and intertestamental writings, we find the term *enemy* referring to three things: personal-political enemies, the people of God in their sin and the devil.

What Is the Christian's Relationship to the Enemy?

As Christians, and not Old Testament Israelites, we must look also at the New Testament for perspective on who our enemies are and how we are to relate to them. The New Testament clearly records that Christians have three enemies: the world, the flesh and the devil.

The world. As Zechariah is moved by the Spirit at the birth of his son, John the Baptist, to announce the salvation that is to come through Jesus Christ, he proclaimed salvation from enemies and the fulfillment of the promise to Abraham (Luke 1:69-75). In a very real sense the promise of God was fulfilled and completed in the person of Jesus Christ. Consequently, in the New Testament personal and political enemies are not depicted so much as *threats* to God's plan but rather as potential *participants* in God's plan. God loves each person and desires that all people come to a knowledge of the Comforter. God longs for our personal and political enemies—even those who despise the Christian faith—to enjoy the blessings of his plan. So instead of praying for their destruction, the New Testament believer is to pray for their salvation (Matthew 5:44; 1 Timothy 2:1-6).

The focus in the New Testament moves from the personal-political enemy to the values and systems that shape people and nations. The New Testament calls this threat to God's plan "the world." This use of the word *world* does not refer so much to a particular person, nation or planet. Rather it identifies human values and structures as they stand against the values of the Creator. Hence the world system—with its oppression, greed, sensuality and so on—is the New Testament enemy. People are not the enemy, but the world system that molds them *is*. Thus John writes, "Do not love the world or the things in the world. The love of the Father is not in those who love the world" (1 John 2:15).

The flesh. The second enemy mentioned in the Old Testament was the people of God themselves as they are against God. How has Jesus' coming affected our relationship with God? The answer is found in Romans 5:10, "For if while we were enemies, we were reconciled to God through the death of his Son, much more surely, having been reconciled, will we be saved by his life." *Enemies reconciled*—that sums it up. We are brought together, made friends. We were once God's enemies, but now through Christ we are made friends. No longer do we need to consider ourselves as enemies insofar as we have been reconciled with Christ.

But we must still reckon with sin in the form of the flesh or our sinful nature. Paul writes, "Live by the Spirit, I say, and do not gratify the desires of the flesh. For what the flesh desires is opposed to the Spirit, and what the Spirit desires is opposed to the flesh" (Galatians 5:16-17). Sin is still opposed to God's plan, even though we ourselves have been reconciled with Christ. In this sense, though we ourselves are not God's enemies, our tendencies toward evil are enemies of God. The power of sin has been crippled through Christ's work on the cross, but we must still fight it fiercely. The focus in the New Testament shifts slightly from God's people insofar as they are against God to the sinful patterns and tendencies which incline us away from God.

The devil. Matthew 13:38-39 refers to Satan as the enemy, the one who sows evil in the midst of God's good work. Like sin, the devil has been defeated by the blood of the Lamb (see Revelation 12:1-12). His end is sure, and his final power is broken. But at present we find that "our struggle is not against enemies of blood and flesh, but against the rulers, against the authorities, against the cosmic powers of this present darkness, against the spiritual forces of evil in the heavenly places" (Ephesians 6:12). The devil and his demonic forces are real. Even though their power has been broken, they still "prowl around looking for someone to devour" (1 Peter 5:8). So the Christian's relationship to the devil, like that to sin, is one of victorious battle: we have the assurance that the war has been won, even though we must still fight battles.

These are the enemies of the Christian—the world, the flesh and the devil. Personal and political opponents have become potential participants in the plan of God, yet the world with its godlessness emerges as enemy. We ourselves as people in sin have been made friends with God through Christ, yet we must face the daily struggle with the flesh. Satan's defeat is sure, yet he is active still.

How Can We Pray These Enemy Psalms?

Now that we know who and what the enemy is, we can move to the practice of Christian warfare: deliverance prayer.

First, it isn't appropriate to reword an enemy psalm into your own words in order to pray that the Lord will destroy those people who ridicule, hate or hurt you. Nor is it appropriate to pray that God will remove all your political opponents. These people are not threats to God's plan but potential participants in his plan. You are to pray for their benefit (Matthew 5:43-47).

You can, however, identify with a phrase in an enemy psalm and pray fervently that the influence of the *world* be destroyed. You can, for example, reflect on the countless, senseless deaths of innocent creatures or on the oppression of the poor, and pray against a world system that allows these atrocities to continue. Psalm 55:15, for example, may inspire a prayer like this: "Let death, O Lord, take our enemy of materialism by surprise. Let the influence of this greedy culture over our lives and our churches go down to Sheol."

Likewise, you can use the enemy psalms to pray against the influence of the *flesh*. There is much to be gained by identifying a particular temptation with which you may struggle and praying an enemy psalm against it. You might say, with Psalm 3, "Rise up, O LORD; deliver me, O my God! Strike my tendencies to gossip and to envy on the cheek; break the teeth, the biting influence of this pattern on my life."

Finally, *Satan* himself may be bound by your prayers. He remains your enemy, and these psalms are wonderful tools with which to bring him down. You may be praying about sharing Christ with a friend, for example, and you want to ask God to frustrate the enemy's deceptive schemes. In your own words you can pray with Psalm 143:12, "In your steadfast love, silence my enemy the devil and all his demonic forces. I pray that their deceptions would not gain an influence over our conversation tonight. Destroy the adversaries, those powers of darkness which would want to accuse and lead my friend away from you. Deliver my friend from the hands of the deceiver. I am your servant tonight."

Despite first appearances, we have found that even the enemy psalms can be worthy models for prayer. We need a new awareness of our enemies today: the world, the flesh and the devil. This awareness is found in understanding the plan of God found in the Scriptures. We need a new hatred for our enemy today. This kind of hatred is found in the language and emotion of the enemy psalms. And last, we need to use powerful tools against the enemy today. We find these tools as we apply warfare and deliverance prayer to specific battles of our lives. The world, the flesh and the devil all continue to oppose God's plan for our life and for the world. By using these psalms as models for our prayers, we can begin to claim ground against these enemies and gain great victories for God's kingdom.

LIST B contains a category of psalms to pray when you wish to express to God your indignation at God's enemies.

10

WHEN PRAYER GOES UNANSWERED

·····································

When our daughter Terese was nine years old, she asked her Sunday-school teacher to pray about her future in art. Terese had been trying to discern whether she was called to be an artist, so at her request, the teacher prayed that God would provide clear direction for her and her art.

Four days later, Terese woke up and told us of a dream she'd had that night. She found herself in a large, beautifully decorated room hung with paintings that she herself had made. She saw herself as a girl of about sixteen looking at her paintings in what was clearly a museum of Christian art. She saw others looking at the art and being inspired toward the gospel. Later, she saw Christ, in a veiled form; and in the midst of her worship, she thanked the glorified Christ for showing her direction for her artwork. As Terese related the dream to us the next morning, she described the experience with a clarity and vividness she had seldom expressed before. Terese understood this dream as a direct answer to her teacher's prayer.

Does God answer prayer? Without a doubt. The Bible clearly promises that God will answer prayer:

Ask, and it will be given you; search, and you will find; knock, and the door will be opened for you. For everyone who asks receives, and everyone who searches, finds, and for everyone who knocks, the door will be opened. (Matthew 7:7-8)

Again, truly I tell you, if two of you agree on earth about anything you ask, it will be done for you by my Father in heaven. (Matthew 18:19)

Whatever you ask for in prayer with faith, you will receive. (Matthew 21:22).

I will do whatever you ask in my name, so that the Father may be glorified in the Son. (John 14:13)

If you abide in me, and my words abide in you, ask for whatever you wish, and it will be done for you. (John 15:7)

You did not choose me but I chose you. And I appointed you to go and bear fruit, fruit that will last, so that the Father will give you whatever you ask him in my name. (John 15:16)

If any of you is lacking in wisdom, ask God, who gives to all generously and ungrudgingly, and it will be given you. (James 1:5)

And we receive from him whatever we ask, because we obey his commandments and do what pleases him. (1 John 3:22)

And this is the boldness we have in him, that if we ask anything according to his will, he hears us. And if we know that he hears us in whatever we ask, we know that we have obtained the requests made of him. (1 John 5:14-15)

These few New Testament examples form a pretty impressive collection! With promises like these our assurance of answered prayer would appear secure. But it doesn't always seem to work out like that in real life, does it?

I remember one Saturday in 1983, when I attended the wedding of a lovely couple as well as the memorial service of a young child. I recall the parents in each service: the bride's so happy, the boy's so sad. The child's parents had prayed and prayed for their son to live. They had solicited the prayers of many friends when they heard the news that their child was sick and might not make it. Yet he died.

We have seen many people experience deep loss despite their fervent prayer: families shattered through trauma or divorce; individuals crippled due to sickness, emotional difficulty or injury; churches crumbled because of division or scandal. Sometimes we pray deeply, sincerely and fervently only to feel that our prayers are somehow not good enough or that God ignores them. Like the psalmist, we cry, "Will you forget me forever?" (Psalm 13:1).

The experience of unanswered prayer can be found even in the pages of Scripture. King David prayed as his son lay sick that the life of his son would be spared. But the son died (2 Samuel 12:15-19). Three times the apostle Paul prayed that a thorn would be removed from his flesh—and three times God refused. Even the Lord Jesus fervently prayed, "Remove this cup from me" (Luke 22:42)—a cup of death he was to drink only hours later.

We feel the pain of unanswered prayer even more keenly when we pray from the Scriptures. Reflecting 2 Peter 3:9, we lift up a prayer of intercession for a friend lost in anger and addictions: "You don't want *any* to perish, Jesus. You want all to come to repentance. Save my friend!" And a week later we discover that our friend was killed in an auto accident, drunk. We pray for a sister with a crippling disease, using our imagination to reflect on Jesus' compassionate desire to heal those who come to him, and we even *see* her healed in our prayers, but our sister does not improve. Instances like these seem to call into question God's own character and Word.

As we see the extravagant promises of answered prayer and the stark reality of unanswered prayer, what is our response? Do we say that God is a liar? Or that he really doesn't care? Or that we are not good enough for God to consider our prayers? I honestly think that these are the explanations that come first to many of us. Of course, we may have heard in Christian circles the old adage that God answers prayer in three ways: yes, no and wait. But sometimes we don't hear God saying yes, no or wait. Sometimes we don't hear *anything* from God, and all we experience is *unanswered* prayer. What will enable us to continue praying the Scriptures after a prayer goes unanswered?

It is my conviction that there are reasonable, biblical explanations for unanswered prayer. Though knowing what Scripture says about prayer will not magically answer all of our "Why, Lord?" questions, it can offer us a sense of confidence and peace as we pursue God in prayer through the difficult circumstances of life. Studying Scripture in this light, we find some issues to explore in two areas: the relationship between God's character and prayer and the broader biblical teaching on prayer.

The Character of God and Prayer

When you feel God is not hearing you, you can remind yourself of the following aspects of his character.

God knows your needs. Psalm 139:1-4 reads, "O LORD, you have searched me and known me. You know when I sit down and when I rise up; you discern my thoughts from far away. You search out my path and my lying down, and are acquainted with all my ways. Even before a word is on my tongue, O LORD, you know it completely." And Jesus in Matthew 6:8 tells us not to pray like the hypocrites: "Do not be like them, for your Father knows what you need before you ask him." God knows your needs. You are praying not to an ignorant or disinterested God but to an all-knowing one.

God loves you. The Bible says God is love. "We love because he first loved us" (1 John 4:19). "God so loved the world that he gave his only Son" (John 3:16). David appeals to the love of God frequently in his prayers. "Turn, O LORD," he says. "Save my soul. Deliver me for the sake of your steadfast love" (Psalm 6:4). Not only does God know your needs, he is also for you. God's desire is that you "might have life, and have it abundantly" (John 10:10). The great Comforter loves you and wants to do what is best for you.

God is powerful. The Almighty rules over all events. Matthew 10:29 says that not even two sparrows fall to the ground apart from the Father's will. In high school I learned a verse on prayer known as God's phone number: "Call to me and I will answer you, and will tell you great and hidden things that you have not known" (Jeremiah 33:3). God asks Moses, "Is the LORD's power limited?" (Numbers 11:23). The God you pray to is not asleep or weak. The powerful One is constantly active, able to act in all the events of your life. The Lord is the Creator. He can create again in your situation. You can trust in God.

God is sovereign. A prayer is not a request of God to alter his eternal purposes or to form new ones. It is simply the taking on of an attitude of active dependence—stating your need honestly and fervently, asking according to God's will and leaving the rest with him. Think of a young girl, just before Christmas. This girl has in mind one particular item she wants very much. She can't buy it herself, nor can she force her parents to buy it. They are the parents, and she is the child. But she can make her desires known—again and again. And her loving parents will most likely get the hint. This is what I mean by *active dependence.* God is the Almighty One. The Lord's will is the central matter in prayer, not your will. God is the Source of life; you are a receiver of life. Yet since he is a gentle and loving Lord, God's desire is to hear your prayers given in a spirit of active dependence.

So what do we find from a look at the relationship between God's character and our prayer? Even when prayers are not answered we can remember these truths. God knows our need; the all-knowing One is not ignorant of our plight. God loves us; like a mother with her child, God does not neglect us. God is powerful; the Almighty rules over all events, including those in our life. We must also remember that God is sovereign and dependent on no one; though God is moved by our prayers, he will be neither controlled nor manipulated.

We are accustomed to getting what we want instantly. We have overnight mail, movies on demand and vending machines offering instant coffee and snacks. At the touch of a button, just about everything can be had instantly—except prayer. God is not a vending machine. We cannot expect to e-mail our request to God and receive an answer moments later through a fax. Prayer is not merely the placing of a request; it is the pursuing of a relationship. We must search for *God* in prayer, not just an answer. When we look at prayer in this way, a lifestyle of praying will result in a lifestyle of receiving.

The Broader Teaching of Scripture on Prayer

By looking at God's character we gain an overall perspective that can help us in our prayers—both answered and unanswered. By seeing what the Scripture says about prayer in general we find specific insights that help us understand the apparent discrepancy between some of the promises we read in the Scriptures and our experience of unanswered prayer.

Scriptural promises concerning prayer should not be taken out of context. Many promises are embedded in passages that are discussing other subjects. A closer look at the promises at the beginning of this chapter shows this. The promise in Matthew 18:19-20 is in the context of a discussion of church discipline. Matthew 21:22 is Jesus' response to the disciples amazement over his cursing of the fig tree. The passages in John are found in a discussion of what to expect when Jesus is gone. The James quotation is found amid an encouragement to seek wisdom. The passages in 1 John give signs of those who are true believers, encouraging them to faithfulness.

Because these authors were addressing issues other than unanswered prayer, the problems related to unanswered prayer simply aren't mentioned. These Scripture references show the fabulous possibilities we have as Christians in prayer. But their promises are not given in the context of a scholarly essay on prayer; the subject of unanswered prayer was simply not relevant to the topics discussed. You cannot look merely to these promises for the whole of God's teaching on prayer.

Scripture does not guarantee results for every single prayer. The encouragement to pray for "whatever" we wish (as in John 15:7) means that you can pray for *anything*—whether big or small, important or unimportant, physical healing or spiritual growth. God will answer *all kinds* of requests. But it does not mean that you are guaranteed to receive *everything*, every individual item for which you pray. The dynamics of relationship with God, the circumstances of the request or even the grace of God may necessitate that a particular prayer not be answered as you might hope. Be careful not to twist the Scriptures to fit a vending-machine approach to answered prayer.

Scripture clearly identifies a variety of factors that promote answered prayer. Without becoming too legalistic, we can label these factors "conditions" for answered prayer. In Jeremiah 29:12-13, the Lord declares, "Then you will call upon me and come and pray to me, and I will hear you. When you search

for me, you will find me; if you seek me with all your heart."
Are you seeking the Lord concerning your request with the
earnestness and wholeheartedness reflected in this passage?
Second Chronicles 7:14 says, "If my people who are called by
my name humble themselves, pray, seek my face and turn
from their wicked ways, then I will hear from heaven, and
will forgive their sin and will heal their land." Are you
pursuing God with a humble and repentant spirit? The
promise in James, mentioned above, reads in full: "If any of
you is lacking in wisdom, ask God who gives to all generously and ungrudgingly, and it will be given you. But ask in
faith never doubting, for the one who doubts is like a wave
of the sea, driven and tossed by the wind" (James 1:5-6). Are
you praying full of doubt or full of faith? The promise in
1 John 3:22 shows the need for obedience in relationship with
God: "We receive from him whatever we ask, because we
obey his commandments and do what pleases him."

Within the dynamics of our relationship with God, these
and other factors cultivate the experience of regularly answered prayer in our lives. If you want to see your prayers
answered more often, I recommend that you aggressively
pursue characteristics like earnestness, humility, repentance,
faith and obedience.

Scripture also names conditions that hinder prayer. To the
idolatrous Israelites, Moses said, "When you returned and
wept before the LORD, the LORD would neither heed your
voice nor pay you any attention" (Deuteronomy 1:45). Likewise Psalm 66:18 says, "If I had cherished iniquity in my
heart, the LORD would not have listened." Proverbs 1:28-31
speaks of how indifference and rejection of God's law affect our

prayer life. Proverbs 21:13 says that whoever closes their ears to the poor will not be heard. James 4:3 speaks of asking and not receiving due to asking selfishly, in order to satisfy our own pleasures. First Peter 3:7 encourages husbands to love their wives so that nothing will hinder their prayers. Thus unconfessed sin, severe rebellion, neglect of the needy, selfish motives—all these can hinder the effectiveness of your prayers.

Scripture describes occasions when God does not answer prayer and does not offer an explanation. Moses, speaking with God in the tabernacle, asks that he might see God's glory in Exodus 33:18. God's response in verse 20 is "You cannot see my face, for no one shall see me and live." The nature of God's character in some mysterious way limits the range of prayers we can ask. In Deuteronomy 3:23-27 Moses begs to pass over the Jordan into the Promised Land, but the Lord is angry with him and does not let him. Job experiences overwhelming tragedy and seeks the Lord time and time again to no avail. Only much later does the Lord see fit to respond to Job's plea. Paul relates in 2 Corinthians 12:7-10 a time when he prayed three times for a difficulty, a "thorn in the flesh," to be removed, and the Lord refused him, instructing him to be satisfied and strengthened in his weakness.

One powerful example of this type of refusal is found in 2 Samuel 12. After Nathan condemns David's wicked deeds of adultery and murder, the Lord strikes David's son ill. David sincerely confesses his sin and repents, as we see in Psalm 51. In addition David seeks the Lord for the child, fasting and lying all night on the ground. David's wholehearted repentance and prayer for the child are clear from the text, yet the

Lord does not answer the prayer as David hopes. The child dies. To his servants' surprise, David gets up from the floor, washes and goes back to work. When the servants question his behavior, he says, "While the child was still alive, I fasted and wept; for I said, 'Who knows? The LORD may be gracious to me, and the child may live.' But now he is dead; why should I fast? Can I bring him back again?" (2 Samuel 12:2-23). David's response shows the depth of his prayers and his active dependency in God's care. He had begged in his prayers, yet deep beneath this fervency was a complete trust in the sovereign God.

In summary, Scripture shows factors that affect both the way we understand promises and the way our prayers are answered. We are reminded, by understanding the contexts of the promise passages and by the intended meaning of the "whatever" language of the promises, that biblical promises ought not to be unduly applied to every prayer. And we have learned that the Bible speaks of a variety of factors which influence God's answer to our prayers. A life increasingly free of vice and full of virtue may foster increased confidence in answered prayer. An unanswered prayer may indicate that God desires us to grow closer. Finally, sometimes God does not answer our prayers, and we have little explanation why. Mystery happens.

Approaching Unanswered Prayer

So how can you approach your experiences of unanswered prayer? Here are a few guidelines based on our study of prayer in Scripture.

1. Be quick to affirm the character of God. The Father loves you; the Spirit knows you; the Almighty is sovereign. God is able to answer your request, and you can trust him. Yet God is not dependent on you. You might want to take Scripture passages proclaiming the character of God (found in LISTS C and D) or stories of Christ (found in LIST E) and soak in thoughts of God's character. Allow your experience of unanswered prayer to be bathed in images of God's character supplied by times of praying the Scriptures.

2. *Examine the promises of Scripture in their own light.* While you need to apply the promises of Scripture to your prayers (see p. 66 and LIST H), be careful not to apply these passages to situations where they do not belong. Try not to overstate or twist the Scriptures to fit your experience. You can only learn to apply the Scriptures correctly when you spend time reading them.

3. *Keep praying.* Like a young child at Christmas, like the persistent friend in Luke 11:5-8, bring your request to the Lord fervently and repeatedly. At times the Lord waits to answer just to draw this persistence from you. At times, as you place your requests before the Lord again and again, you will notice elements of the request or of your approach to God that need "refinement." After accomplishing his work in your heart and in your request, God can then look at both and say, "Now I am ready to answer so that all may rejoice." Persistence in prayer will cultivate the transformation from merely seeking the object of your requests in prayer to seeking *the Lord* in prayer.

4. *Self-examination.* If after persistent prayer you are not experiencing what you expected, examine yourself. Are you harboring sins or omitting something (or someone) from your Christian practice? We learned about self-examination in chapter eight, and these methods of praying the Scriptures (and the

passages in LIST I) can help you search your soul. You need not be slavishly introspective, certain that the problem in prayer is due to your own sin. Simply allow the Lord to show you if your prayers are being hindered by some matter in your own walk.

5. *Trust God.* Finally, always approach God with a sense of trust in his mystery and sovereignty. Your prayer requests are not vending-machine quarters which you plug into God, expecting to find your answers instantly popping out. No, just ask and keep on asking. And as you take on a lifestyle of asking, you will experience a lifestyle of receiving.

Just as Jesus encouraged his disciples not to be afraid of his departure but to lay hold of the benefits made available to them in his absence, so God encourages us not to be afraid of him but to make use of the power available in prayer.

So *pray!* Whether on your knees or sitting in your chair, become like the widow who repeatedly knocked on the judge's door. Pound on those gates of heaven! Be confident! You are Jesus' friend, and you are in the presence of the God who is eager to give you whatever you ask. Don't be discouraged by unanswered prayer. Instead, remember the character of God, understand the context of the Scriptures, examine your soul and transcend the times of unanswered prayer to an ever-deepening relationship with God.

The methods of praying the Scriptures you now know will help you. Many believers have pressed through to lives of deep and effective prayer. By God's grace you can too.

PART 2

A GUIDE
TO SCRIPTURES
FOR PRAYER

*"FOR THINE IS THE KINGDOM
AND THE POWER AND THE GLORY
FOREVER AND EVER! AMEN."*

LIST A

PRAYING THE
LORD'S PRAYER

·····································

For Use with Chapter Two

This chart outlines the main types of prayer as they are presented in the Lord's Prayer. Use this outline to guide you through a time of prayer using these main types.

Verse from Lord's Prayer	How to Pray	Type of Prayer
Our Father who art in heaven, Hallowed be thy name.	Telling God how great he is and how much he means to you.	Worship, thanksgiving
Thy kingdom come, Thy will be done, On earth as it is in heaven.	Giving God total control over all the areas in your (or another's) life.	Submission, surrender
Give us this day our daily bread;	Asking God to provide for the day's needs.	Petition, intercession
And forgive us our debts, As we also have forgiven our debtors;	Admitting your sin to God and asking for forgiveness; telling God how you have been sinned against and forgiving those who have hurt you.	Confession

Verse from Lord's Prayer	How to Pray	Type of Prayer
And lead us not into temptation, But deliver us from evil.	Asking God to give you (or another) strength over particular areas of evil to which you (or another) fall prey.	Supplication, Deliverance

LIST B

PSALMS LISTED BY MOOD

....

For Use with Chapters Three and Nine

The following chart lists categories that reflect the variety of emotions and circumstances of both the Psalms and our own lives. As you begin your time of prayer, choose the category which best suits your need or emotional state. To the right of the category, you will find a list of psalms that serve to express that sentiment. My favorite psalms in each category are indicated in bold.

Category	Psalm
Your contemplative meditations	8, **19**, 36, 68, **77**, 87, 89, 90, 114, 132
Your adoration for who God is	8, 11, 23, 24, 67, 75, 84, **93**, 95, 96, 97, **100**, 117, 134, 139, 145, 146, **147**, 148, 149, 150
Your worship for what God has done in creation and preservation	33, 66, 76, 98, 99, **104, 105**, 108, 124, **135**, 136
Your praise and worship for what God continues to do	27, 29, **46**, 47, 65, **103**, 104, **111**, 113, 121
Your thanksgiving for what God has done for you (answered prayer)	9, **18**, 21, **30**, 34, 40, 48, 66, 92, **107**, 116, 118, 126, 138
Your submission to God	16, 25, 27, 56, **62**, 71, **101, 131**

Category	Psalm
Your hope in the Messiah	2, **16**, 45, **110**
Your confidence in the law	**1**, 19, 50, **119**
Your meditations on wise sayings	1, **14, 15**, 37, **49**, 53, 91, 112, 125, 127, 133
Your struggle with temptation (also try the section on enemy psalms below with your temptation as the enemy)	**73, 141**
Your desire for guidance from the Lord, or your worry	5, **25, 27**, 61, 143
Confession and sorrow for sin	6, **32, 51**, 106, 130
Your distress or need in general	3, 4, 5, 7, **17**, 28, 43, 54, 57, 59, 70, **86**, 108, **123**, 144
Your prayers for the needs of another	**20**, 72, 85, 115, 122, **128**
Your pain or frustration in a time of illness	6, **38**, 41, **88, 102**
Your discouragement or hurt	**13**, 22, 26, **42**, 60, 69, 74, 79, **142**
Your sorrow or hope near death	**23**, 31, **39**, 63, 88, 143
Your grief or mourning	6, 31, **77, 137**
Your expression of God's righteous anger at his people	**49, 50, 78, 81**, 82
Your indignation at God's enemies (enemy psalms; see also chapter nine)	10, 12, **35**, 40, 52, **55**, 58, 64, **69**, 83, 94, 109, 120, 129, 140
Your anger at God	**44, 80**, 137

LIST C

SCRIPTURE PASSAGES FOR WORSHIP & THANKSGIVING

....

For Use with Chapter Four

This list identifies some of the passages cultivating worship and thanksgiving as they are found in the Old and New Testament. They are arranged by type of passage and location in the Bible to make it easy to find a passage you might want to pray. My favorite samples of each type are highlighted in bold.

Visions of and Encounters with God in the Old Testament
These are good for rekindling your own vision of God or identifying with others' encounters with the Lord.

The covenant of the Lord with Abram .... Genesis 15:12-18
Jacob's dream .... Genesis 28:10-17
Moses and the burning bush .... Exodus 3:1—4:17
Moses meets with God on Mt. Sinai .... Exodus 24:15-18
God shows Moses his glory .... Exodus 33:18-23
Elijah meets the Lord on a mountain .... 1 Kings 19:1-18
Elijah is taken up to heaven .... 2 Kings 2: 9-12
Isaiah meets the Lord .... Isaiah 6:1-8
Ezekiel's visions of the Lord .... Ezekiel 1:2-28; 10:1-22;
                                                                                                          43:1-12

Daniel's vision of the four animals .... Daniel 7:1-14
Daniel's vision of a man.. **Daniel 10:4-19**

Special Times of Worship in the Old Testament
These passages are good for fostering powerful times of meeting with God.

The tent of meeting..Exodus 33:7-17
Aaron and his sons offer sacrifices .... **Leviticus 9:22-24**
God destroys Aaron's sons who worshiped
   without regard for the Lord's holiness..............................Leviticus 10:1-3
David dances before the Lord.. **2 Samuel 6:12-23**
Ezra reads the book of Moses .... Nehemiah 8:1-12

Worship Hymns in the Old Testament (see also the list of the Psalms, pp. 113-14)
Here are a few hymns of worship to use in your own worship.

The returned captives worship God.................................... **Nehemiah 9:5-38**
Job's response to the Lord's speech .... Job 42:1-6
Praise of God as a beloved one............................... **Song of Solomon 2:3-6;**
                                                     7:10-13
A song of praise .... Isaiah 42:10-13
A short worship hymn... Jeremiah 16:19-20

Thanksgivings in the Old Testament (see also the list of the Psalms, pp. 113-14)
Here are a few prayers of thanksgiving. Use these to help you form your own words of thanksgiving to God.

Moses' song of thanksgiving ....Exodus 15:1-18
Deborah's song of victory ....**Judges 5:1-31**
Hannah's prayer of thanks...1 Samuel 2:1-10
David's praise for God's protection....................................2 Samuel 22:1-51
David's thanks at the ark's return .... **1 Chronicles 16:8-36**

Praise at the rebuilding of the temple
  foundation .... Ezra 3:10-11
Thanksgiving when God restores fellowship .... Isaiah 12:1-6
Praise for deliverance from oppression .... Isaiah 25:1-5
Hezekiah's thanks for healing...**Isaiah 38:10-20**
A song of happiness ....Isaiah 61:1-11
Daniel's praise for wisdom .... Daniel 2:19-23

Worship of Jesus in the Gospels

Here are some portraits of people who worshiped Jesus. Imagine yourself in their place, and allow your own worship of Jesus to arise.

The wise men worship the child Jesus .... **Matthew 2:1-12**
The shepherds worship the newborn Savior .... Luke 2:8-20
The baptism of Jesus .... Matthew 3:13-17; Mark
                                                                                            1:9-11; Luke 3:21-22;
                                                                                            John 1:29-34
The miraculous catch of fish .... Luke 5:1-11
A woman brings ointment...**Luke 7:36-50**
Jesus walks on water...Matthew 14:22-33
Peter's declaration of Christ ....Matthew 16:13-20;
                                                                                            Mark 8:27-30; Luke 9:18-21;
                                                                                            cf. John 6:67-69
The transfiguration .... **Matthew 17:1-9;**
                                                                                            Mark 9:2-10; Luke 9:28-36
Jesus heals a man born blind ....John 9:1-41
Mary's anointing of Jesus at Bethany .... Matthew 26:6-13;
                                                                                            Mark 14:3-9; John 12:1-8
Jesus' triumphal entry into Jerusalem   **Matthew 21:1-11;**
                                                                                            Mark 11:1-10; Luke 19:28-40;
                                                                                            John 12:12-19
The soldiers' mock worship at Jesus' trial ....Matthew 27:27-31;
                                                                                            Mark 15:16-20; John 19:1-16
The admiration of the centurion at Jesus' .... Matthew 27:45-54;
  death .... Mark 15:33-39;
                                                                                            Luke 23:44-48
The women meet the resurrected Jesus .... **Matthew 28:1-10**
Mary Magdalene meets the resurrected Jesus...............................John 20:1-18
Jesus appears to Thomas and others ....John 20:24-29

The disciples worship the resurrected
  Christ ....Matthew 28:16-20

Spirit-Led Worship in the Book of Acts

*These portraits of the worship of the early church filled with the
Holy Spirit inspire our own Spirit-led worship.*

The coming of the Holy Spirit...**Acts 2:1-13**
The church prays after a warning... Acts 4:23-31
Saul meets the Lord...**Acts 9:1-19**
The Gentiles receive the Holy Spirit .... Acts 10:34-48
Paul and Barnabas are set apart for a mission................................. Acts 13:1-3
Paul and Silas praise God in a jail cell ....**Acts 16:22-28**
Some followers of John the Baptist receive
  the Spirit... Acts 19:1-7
Late-night worship leads to a miraculous
  healing... Acts 20:7-12

Hymns and Benedictions in the Epistles

*These are some of the earliest Christian hymns and formal prayers
of the church. They are great for public prayer of the Scriptures.*

A doxology...Romans 16:25-27
The humility of Christ...**Philippians 2:6-11**
The supremacy of Christ ....Colossians 1:15-20
Glory to the King of the ages ....1 Timothy 1:17
The mystery of Christ ....1 Timothy 3:16
Honor to the Lord of lords ....1 Timothy 6:15-16
A benediction ....**Jude 24-25**

Some Thanksgivings in the Epistles

*Here are more prayers offering thanksgiving to God for what he has
provided.*

The Roman Christians' faith...Romans 1:8-10
Grace and strengthening from God................................. 1 Corinthians 1:4-6

Victory through Christ... 1 Corinthians 15:57
Consolation in affliction.................................**2 Corinthians 1:3-6**
Titus' eagerness for missionary work.........................2 Corinthians 8:16-17
Spiritual blessings through Christ .... Ephesians 1:3
The Philippian saints' participation
   in the gospel ....**Philippians 1:3-6**
The Colossian believers' faith and love................................ Colossians 1:3-5
The Thessalonians' faith, hope and love..................**1 Thessalonians 1:2-3**
Timothy's sincere faith in Christ .... 2 Timothy 1:2-5
Philemon's love for the saints and faith in
   Christ .... Philemon 4-6

Pictures of Worship in the Book of Revelation

Here are some awesome pictures of the almighty God in heaven.
These images of worship inspire praise and adoration of the God
who is sovereign over all. A vision of heaven makes the troubles of
this world seem quite small.

One like the Son of Man .... Revelation 1:9-20
John sees heaven...**Revelation 4:1-11**
The vision of the Lamb .... Revelation 5:1-14
A great crowd worships God... Revelation 7:9-17
Worship at the seventh trumpet..................................... Revelation 11:15-19
The song of the 144,000.. Revelation 14:1-5
A victory song and the seven disasters .... Revelation 15:2-8
People in heaven praise God ....**Revelation 19:1-10**
The vision of the new Jerusalem .... Revelation 21:1—22:5

LIST D

THEOLOGICAL MEDITATION

....

For Use with Chapter Five

This list presents a selection of significant passages relating to the main themes or doctrines of the Christian faith. You may wish to supplement this list of passages related to your theme by looking in a concordance or some other reference.

How God Makes Himself Known
Psalm 8:1-9; Acts 17:22-31; Romans 1:18-25; 2:14-16

How God Reveals Salvation
Exodus 14:1-30; 1 Kings 18:17-40; Jeremiah 1:4-10; John 10:31-38; 2 Timothy 3:16; Hebrews 1:1-2; 2 Peter 1:20-21

What God Is Like
Genesis 1:1-31; Exodus 3:13-15; Numbers 11:1; Psalm 84:1-2; 93:1-5; 147:1-20; John 4:24.

God's Knowledge
Job 21:22; Psalm 94:8-11; 139:1-18; Matthew 7:28-29; John 1:43-51

God's Power
Exodus 15:1-7; Numbers 16:23-35; Psalm 68:32-35; Mark 5:35-42; Ephesians 1:17-23

God's Holiness
Exodus 3:1-6; Isaiah 6:1-5; 1 Peter 1:13-16; Revelation 4:1-11

God's Love
Psalm 136:1-26; Hosea 11:1-4; John 3:16; 1 John 4:7-19

God's Character as Father, Son and Holy Spirit
Matthew 28:19; 1 Corinthians 12:5-7; 2 Corinthians 13:13; 1 Peter 1:2;
Jude 20-21

God's Creation
Genesis 1:1—2:3; Psalm 33:6-9; John 1:1-4; Romans 8:18-22

Humanity as the Image of God
Genesis 1:26—2:25; 5:1-2; Psalm 8:4-8; Ephesians 4:22-24

The Tragedy of Sin
Genesis 3:1-24; Psalm 51:1-5; Isaiah 64:4-9; Mark 7:17-23; Romans 1:18-32; 3:9-20; James 1:12-16

The Law
Exodus 20:1-17; Deuteronomy 6:1-9; Psalm 119:1-176; Matthew 5:17-20;
Romans 7:1—8:8; 10:4

The Person of Jesus Christ (see also list E, Gospel Meditation)
Luke 9:18-22; John 1:1-18; Acts 10:34-43; Philippians 2:5-11; Colossians
1:13-20; Hebrews 4:14-15

The Death of Christ on the Cross and Its Meaning for Us
Isaiah 53:1-12; Matthew 27:1-66; Mark 15:16-47; Luke 23:26-56; John
19:16-42; Romans 5:6-11; Colossians 2:13-15; Hebrews 9:11-14; 12:1-3

The Resurrection of Our Lord and Its Meaning for Us
Matthew 28:1-20; Mark 16:1-19; Luke 24:1-53; John 11:25-26; 20:1-31;
Romans 4:25; 6:1-9; 8:11; 1 Corinthians 15:12-28; Ephesians 1:20-22; Revelation 1:17-18

Receiving Salvation Through Repentance and Faith
Matthew 4:17; John 3:1-16; Acts 2:37-39; Romans 10:9-13; 1 Corinthians
6:9-11; Ephesians 2:5-10; 1 Peter 1:8-9

The Holy Spirit
Genesis 1:1-2; Numbers 11:24-25; Ezekiel 36:22-32; Luke 4:1-19; John 14:15-31; 15:26—16:15; Acts 2:1-21, 38; Ephesians 1:13-14

Christian Life in the Spirit (see also passages on self-examination in chapter eight)
Matthew 3:11-12; Luke 4:1; Romans 6:12-23; 8:1-39; Galatians 5:13-26; 6:7-10; 1 Peter 1:10-16; 5:6-11

The Church of God
Matthew 16:13-20; 18:15-20; Acts 6:1-6; 15:1-29; 1 Corinthians 12:1—14:40; 1 Timothy 2:1—3:16; Titus 1:5-9; 1 Peter 5:1-5; Revelation 3:1-22

Our Eternal Life and Resurrection after Death
1 Corinthians 15:35-58; 2 Corinthians 4:13—5:10; 1 Thessalonians 4:13-18; Revelation 20:4-6

The Return of Christ and the End of All Things
Matthew 24—25; Mark 13:1-37; 1 Thessalonians 5:1-11; 2 Thessalonians 2:1-12; 2 Peter 3:1-14; Revelation 1—22

LIST E

GOSPEL MEDITATION

··

For Use with Chapter Five

This list presents passages that are especially helpful for meditating on the life of Jesus, as recorded in the Gospels. It is organized by themes or aspects of God's character as seen in the life of Christ. Under the heading of each theme are listed a number of stories with their locations in each of the Gospels given on the right. It is sometimes helpful to read the story in more than one Gospel before proceeding with meditation.

Theme	Matthew	Mark	Luke	John
Jesus' Divinity				
Jesus' birth	1:18-25		2:1-52	
Jesus' baptism	3:13-17	1:9-11	3:21-22	1:29-37
Jesus' transfiguration	17:1-13	9:2-13	9:28-36	
The triumphal entry	21:1-11	11:1-11	19:28-44	12:12-19
The death of Christ	27:32-61	15:21-47	23:26-56	19:16-42
The resurrection	28:1-10	16:1-8	24:1-12	20:1-18
Jesus Recruits and Leads Followers				
The call of the disciples	4:18-22	1:16-20	5:1-11	1:35-51
		3:13-19	6:12-16	
The calling of Matthew	9:9-12	2:13-17	5:27-32	
Jesus sends out the Twelve	10:1-42	6:6-13	9:1-6	
Peter's declaration	16:13-20	8:27-30	9:18-20	
The calling of Zacchaeus			19:1-10	

Theme	Matthew	Mark	Luke	John
Jesus Recruits and Leads Followers				
The road to Emmaus			24:13-49	
Jesus shares fish with Peter				21:4-19
Jesus' Encouragement to Those Who Believe				
The Canaanite woman's faith	15:21-28	7:24-30		
Jesus anointed at Bethany	26:6-13	14:3-9		12:1-11
Jesus anointed by a sinner			7:36-50	
The return of the seventy-two			10:17-24	
Jesus appears to Thomas				20:24-31
Christ's Holy Demands				
The cost of following Jesus	8:18-22		9:57-62 14:25-33	
A clean heart	15:1-20	7:1-23		
The rich young ruler	19:16-30	10:17-31	18:18-30	
Nicodemus must be reborn				3:1-21
Jesus' Wisdom and Authority in Tough Interpersonal Situations				
The boy Jesus in the temple			2:41-52	
John the Baptist's question	11:1-19		7:18-35	
Seating in heaven	20:20-28	10:35-45		
Jesus answers Jewish leaders	22:15-46	12:13-40	20:20-47	
Jesus' Love				
Jesus blesses children	19:13-14	9:33-50	18:15-17	
The Last Supper	26:17-30	14:12-31	22:1-38	13:1-38
Martha and Mary			10:38-42	
A Samaritan woman				4:1-42
The high priestly prayer				17:1-26

Theme	Matthew	Mark	Luke	John
Jesus' Compassion				
Healing a woman and a girl	9:18-26	5:21-43	8:40-56	
Feeding five thousand	14:13-21	6:30-44	9:10-17	6:1-15
Feeding four thousand	15:32-39	8:1-10		
The blind receive sight	20:29-34	10:46-52	18:35-43	
The blind man at Bethsaida		8:22-26		
Jesus raises a widow's son			7:11-17	
Jesus' sorrow for Jerusalem			13:31-35	
Jesus at the Pharisee's house			14:1-14	
Healing at the pool of Siloam				5:1-15
Jesus' Forgiving Welcome				
The healing of a paralytic	9:1-8	2:1-12	5:17-26	
Jesus anointed at Bethany	26:6-13	14:3-9		12:1-8
Jesus anointed by a sinner			7:36-50	
Ten healed of leprosy			17:11-19	
Jesus welcomes Zacchaeus			19:1-10	
Jesus' Just Wrath				
Woes on unrepentant cities	11:20-24		10:13-16	
Jesus clears the temple	21:12-17	11:15-19	19:45-48	2:13-25
On the scribes and Pharisees	23:1-36			
Jesus' Power and Authority				
The calming of the storm	8:23-27	4:35-41	8:22-25	
Jesus and Beelzebub	12:22-37	3:20-30	11:14-26	
Jesus walks on water	14:22-36	6:45-52		6:16-21
Jesus' authority questioned	21:23-27	11:27-33	20:1-8	
A demon obeys Jesus		1:21-28	4:31-37	
Demons sent into swine	8:28-34	5:1-20	8:26-39	
Jesus turns water into wine				2:1-11
Lazarus is raised to life				11:1-44
Jesus Faces Temptation				
The devil tempts Christ	4:1-11	1:12-13	4:1-13	
An attempt to make him king				6:15

Peter's declaration	16:21-23	8:27-30		
At Gethsemane	26:36-46	14:32-42	22:39-46	

Theme	Matthew	Mark	Luke	John
Jesus Faces Rejection				
Rejected at his hometown			4:14-30	
Addresses sabbath issues	12:1-14	2:23-27	6:1-11	
Disciples begin to desert him				6:60-69
He is betrayed	26:1-25	14:10-21	22:1-23	13:21-30
Captured at the garden	26:47-56	14:43-52	22:47-53	18:1-12
Peter denies his Lord	26:57-75	14:66-72	22:54-62	18:15-27
Jesus Faces Suffering and Death				
The trials	27:1-31	14:53-65	22:63-71	18:14-40
		15:1-20	23:1-25	19:1-16
The crucifixion and burial	27:32-61	15:21-47	23:26-56	19:16-42

LIST F

PRAYING FOR PERSONAL & CORPORATE NEEDS

For Use with Chapter Six

This list contains a collection of passages to help you to find words for your requests, and to get a feel for the prayers and pray-ers of the Scriptures. Nearly all of these passages are petitions or intercessions themselves, although some mention but do not present the prayer. A few remained unanswered. I have tried to arrange them into categories that reflect the types of prayer both as they are found in the Scriptures and as one might have need of them. Again, favorites are highlighted in bold. I have given other suggestions concerning how to pray these types of prayers in chapter one.

Simple Old Testament Requests (see also LIST B on the Psalms, pp. 113-14)

Isaiah 38:1-3
A cupbearer prays for help ....Nehemiah 1:4-11
A tired laborer prays for strength .... Nehemiah 6:9
Isaiah prays for himself and the nation .... Isaiah 26:7-19
Jeremiah prays for mercy .... Jeremiah 10:23-25

A Few Interesting Conversations with the Lord

Abraham bargains with God about Sodom .... Genesis 18:17-33
Moses debates about his calling ....Exodus 3:1—4:17
Samuel talks with God about anointing a king .... 1 Samuel 16:1-3
Solomon prays for wisdom...1 Kings 3:1-15;
2 Chronicles 1:7-13
Elijah talks to God in hiding ....1 Kings 19:4-18
Isaiah sees the Lord ....Isaiah 6:1-11

People Plead to Jesus for Themselves or for Others

A leper begs for help ....Matthew 8:2; Mark
1:40; Luke 5:12
The disciples cry out in a storm.............................. Matthew 8:25; Luke 8:24
The blind call for help...Matthew 9:27; 20:30;
Mark 10:46-52;
Luke 18:35-43
People plead for a miracle...John 6:30-31
A man asks to know the Son of Man.. John 9:35-38
Jairus pleads for his daughter.. Mark 5:21-23
Demons beg not to be tortured.. Luke 8:28
The Canaanite woman pleads for her daughter.............Matthew 15:21-28;
Mark 7:26-30
An official intercedes for his son..John 4:46-50
A son with an evil spirit..Mark 9:17-24;
Luke 9:38-40
A centurion pleads in faith for his servant ....Matthew 8:5-9;
Luke 7:6-8
Ten lepers cry for mercy ....Luke 17:12-13
A mother displays her ambitions for her sons.................Matthew 20:20-23;
Mark 10:35-40
Peter begs to be washed by Jesus... John 13:9

Paul's Prayers for Others

Unity ....Romans 15:5-6
Hope ....Romans 15:13
The glory of the inheritance... **Ephesians 1:15-21**
Knowledge of God's love ....Ephesians 3:14-21
Blamelessness, fruitfulness, discerning love ....Phillippians 1:9-11
Knowledge of God's will, strength for
   endurance...Colossians 1:9-12
Knit together in love, assured understanding ....Colossians 2:1-3
Increasing love and holiness... 1 Thessalonians
                                  3:11-13
Sanctification and soundness .... 1 Thessalonians
                                  5:23-24
Worthiness and fulfillment.. 2 Thessalonians
                                  1:11-12
Comfort... 2 Thessalonians
                                  2:16-17
Love and patience.. 2 Thessalonians 3:5
Peace .... 2 Thessalonians 3:16

A Few Ceremonial Prayers

The Aaronic blessing..**Numbers 6:22-27**
David's prayer at the temple offerings.........................1 Chronicles 29:10-19
Solomon's dedication of the temple.................................**1 Kings 8:22-53;**
                                  2 Chronicles 6:12-42
Hezekiah prays for forgiveness of his people.............2 Chronicles 30:18-20

Leaders Pray for the Lord's Work

Moses and Joshua pray for a wandering people.
Moses brings water from a rock ....Exodus 17:4-7
Moses asks for the Lord's presence to go with him ....Exodus 33:12-17
Moses prays for the people after they worship
   the golden calf.. **Exodus 32:11-14,**
                                   31-32; 34:9;
                                  Deuteronomy 9:18-29
Moses prays when traveling from Sinai ....Numbers 10:35;
                                    cf. Exodus 15:22-25;
                                    17:8-13; Deuteronomy
                                    10:10

Moses prays for the grumbling community............... Numbers 11:1-2; 10-15
Moses prays for Miriam's disease... Numbers 12:13
Moses prays for the people after the report on
   the Promised Land .... Numbers 14:13-19
Moses prays after God sends poisonous snakes..................... Numbers 21:7
Moses prays for a successor... Numbers 27:15-17
Joshua's prayer after the defeat of Ai .... Joshua 7:6-9

David and others pray for themselves or others.
David seeks direction in battle and in peace............... 1 Samuel 23:2, 10-11;
                                                                                                    30:8; 2 Samuel 2:1;
                                                                                                    5:19
David prays for his descendants .... **2 Samuel 7:18-29;**
                                                                                                    1 Chronicles
                                                                                                    17:16-27
David's prayer during the three-day plague .... 2 Samuel 24:17
Solomon prays for wisdom... 1 Kings 3:1-15;
                                                                                                    2 Chronicles 1:7-12
Elijah prays for fire from the Lord .... 1 Kings 18:36-37
Asa prays as an army comes against him......................... 2 Chronicles 14:11
Jehoshaphat's prayer for help in distress .... 2 Chronicles 20:5-12
Hezekiah's prayer for deliverance .... **2 Kings 19:14-19;**
                                                                                                    Isaiah 37:14-20
Nehemiah prays about his opponents .... Nehemiah 4:4-5; 6:14
Jesus prays for himself, his disciples and
   all believers.. John 17:1-26

A Few Complaints to God
Joshua complains to God after a defeat .... Joshua 7:6-9
Job raises his case against God.................................... Job 23:1-17; 29:1-31:40
Jeremiah raises a series of complaints .... Jeremiah 12:1-4;
                                                                                                    15:15-18; 17:14-18;
                                                                                                    18:19-23; 20:17-18
Jonah complains about his success at Nineveh .... Jonah 4:1-11
Habakkuk complains to God about the nations .... Habakkuk 1:2-4, 12-17

A note about surrender: While God's people voice serious complaints to God, it
appears that they do so in a context of surrender, as in the following prayers.
Job's prayer of surrender.. Job 1:21
Habakkuk's surrender to God .... Habakkuk 3:1-19

Prayers and Requests for Prayer Related to Evangelistic Outreach

Prayers for Healing Prior to the Ministry of Healing

LIST G

PRAYERS FOR
MERCY & REVIVAL

....

For Use with Chapter Seven

The following passages of Scripture are especially good for use in personal and group times of praying for mercy and revival.

Revival Prayers in the Old Testament

Prophetic Psalms

Revival Prayers in the New Testament

LIST H

A FEW PROMISES
TO USE IN PRAYER

....

For Use with Chapter Seven

Here is a brief list of promises in different categories.

Promises of Relationship with God
If you seek God, you will find him ....Deuteronomy 4:29
He will be your God, and you will be his people .... **Genesis 17:7-8;**
Jeremiah 30:22;
Ezekiel 36:28;
Revelation 21:3, 7
God is like a husband...Hosea 2:14-23;
Revelation 21:2
God is your friend ....John 15:12-15
He will be with you always ....Matthew 28:19-20
You have an eternal home...John 14:1-2

Promises of Forgiveness to Those Who Confess
The Lord forgives ....Psalm 130:3-4
Forgive others and you will be forgiven.....................................Matthew 6:14
In Christ you have forgiveness..Ephesians 1:7
If you confess your sins, God will forgive.......................................**1 John 1:9**

Promises of Care in Trials and Temptations
Suffering is temporary..Psalm 30:5
God protects you during trials..Isaiah 43:2
All things work together for good ....**Romans 8:28-39**
No temptation is too great to endure............................ **1 Corinthians 10:13**

Affliction prepares you for eternal glory .... 2 Corinthians 4:17
In the end God will deliver you from all sorrow .... Revelation 21:4

Promises for the Church
The gates of hell will not prevail against you .... Matthew 16:18
You can accomplish great works .... John 14:12
The Holy Spirit empowers you to witness .... Acts 1:8
Believers will demonstrate God's wisdom
to supernatural powers .... Ephesians 3:10
Christ leads the church .... Ephesians 4:15; 5:23;
Colossians 1:18
Christ will conquer our adversary Satan .... Revelation 12:10-13

Promises of Salvation for Those Who Turn to the Lord
The Lord is the deliverer .... Psalm 34:19-20
The Lord will save you .... Zephaniah 3:17
Jesus is the bread of life .... John 6:35
The gospel as the power of salvation .... **Romans 1:16**
Believe, confess and you will be saved .... Romans 10:9-13

Promises of Answered Prayer (see also chapter ten)
Call, and the Lord will answer .... Isaiah 58:9
Pray believing, and you will receive .... Matthew 21:22
Ask, and you will receive .... **Luke 11:9**
Abide in God, ask what you will .... John 15:7
Ask according to God's will, and he hears you .... 1 John 5:14-15

LIST I

COMMANDMENTS & SCRIPTURAL EXHORTATIONS

....

For Use with Chapter Eight

These are larger portions of Scripture. Use them to identify areas in your life the Lord desires to transform. Portions of the Old Testament law are best understood with help from a commentary or a well-informed friend or pastor.

The Ten Commandments
Exodus 20:1-17
Deuteronomy 5:6-21

The Old Testament Law
Exodus 21—23; 25—30; 31:12-17
Leviticus 1—7; 11—27
Numbers 5—6; 15; 28—30
Deuteronomy 5—28

Exhortations in Acts
Acts 15:22-29; 20:17-35

Some Encouragements to Christlike Living in the Letters
Romans 12—15
1 Corinthians 5—8; 10—14

Galatians 5—6
Ephesians 4—6
Philippians 2—4
Colossians 2:6—4:6
1 Thessalonians 4—5
2 Thessalonians 3:6-15
1 Timothy 5—6
2 Timothy 2:14-26
Titus 3:1-11
Hebrews 3:7—4:16; 6:1-12; 10:19-39; 12:1—13:17
James, 1-2 Peter, 1-3 John, Jude (all of them)

The Letters to the Seven Churches in Revelation
Revelation 2:1—3:22